Elizabeth Foy Larsen

111 Places
in the Twin Cities
That You Must
Not Miss

emons:

© Photographs: Elizabeth Foy Larsen Larsen, except:
The Landing (ch. 55): Three Rivers Park District;
Luminary Loppet (ch. 57): Steve Kotvis, f/go, (www.f-go.us)

Art Credits: 35 W Bridge Remembrance Garden (ch. 2): Oslund and Associates;
6th Avenue SE Gateway (ch. 3): Aldo Moroni "Sixth Avenue Stroll,"
Commissioned by the City of Minneapolis, Art in Public Places;
Bob Dylan Mural (ch. 11): Eduardo Kobra, Hennepin Theater Trust;
Can Can Wonderland (ch. 13): Eric Fetrow and Matt Carlyle "You Gotta
Have Heart"; Dred and Harreit Scott (ch. 25): Courtesy of the Minnesota
Historical Society; House of Balls (ch. 44): Allen Christian; Ingebretsen's (ch. 46):
Judith Kjenstad; Manhole Covers (ch. 59): David Atkinson; Minneapolis American
Indian Center (ch. 68): George Morrison; Open Book (ch. 78): Karen Wirth
"Gail See Staircase"; Union Depot (ch. 103) Ray King "Twin Waves";
Zoran Mojsilov Sculptures (ch. 111): Zoran Mojsilov

© Cover motif: private
Design: Eva Kraskes, based on a design
by Lübbeke | Naumann | Thoben
Maps: altancicek.design, www.altancicek.de
Printing and binding: Grafisches Centrum Cuno, Calbe
Printed in Germany 2021
ISBN 978-3-7408-1347-5
Revised second edition, May 2021

Did you enjoy it? Do you want more?
Join us in uncovering new places around the world on:
www.111places.com

Foreword

In 1984, I dropped out of an East Coast college and moved home to Minneapolis, the city where I'd grown up swimming in the same lakes I'd skate on in winter. I rented an apartment in the Wedge, the historic but tattered neighborhood where some of The Replacements lived. I bussed tables at the Monte Carlo in a part of downtown that would one day become the epicenter of loft living and tasting menus. And I did odd jobs, including working as an extra in Prince's concert scenes filmed at First Avenue for "Purple Rain."

I also ventured across the river to St. Paul, Minneapolis's more reserved and older sibling, where I lost myself in the stacks at the late great Hungry Mind Bookstore and developed a taste for Afghani cuisine at Khyber Pass Café. I biked Mississippi River Boulevard and savored the views of the iconic river.

I didn't realize that every one of these places would become part of the Twin Cities' living history. All I knew was that Minneapolis and St. Paul would take care of me while I sorted myself out.

Since that rough start, I've lived in and visited many different cities around the world. And during that time, the world has come to Minnesota. Today, the greater metro area is a dynamic mix of the descendants of our original Dakota residents and German and Scandinavian settlers, alongside thriving Hmong and Latino communities and the largest Somali diaspora in North America.

This book is a love letter to the places that make up this constantly evolving metro area, from a tool library, to James J. Hill's mansion, to the largest walkable art experience in the country. You'll discover an historic curling club, a GLBT library that actually started in a closet, and the lesser-known gems of our world-class theater scene. Most of all, you'll venture outdoors and revel in the idea that in this special northern spot, nature meets culture like no other city in America.

E.F.L.

111 Places

1__331 Club

A neighborhood bar with bonus points

In 1884, an ordinance was enacted in Minneapolis that severely limited where saloons could operate. Much of Northeast, however, fell outside that jurisdiction, which is why the area has long been a hotbed for neighborhood bars. One of the oldest is the 331 Club, which first opened in 1899 on the corner of 13th Avenue NE and University Avenue.

An old-fashioned bar and live-music venue, the 331 Club got a new start in 2005, when, after being for sale for years, it was purchased by hair salon and art gallery-owner Jon Oulman and his son, Jarret, who gussied it up just enough to inject a shot of chic into the dive-bar vibe. They uncovered the original tin ceilings, now painted navy blue, built a stage, and updated the kitchen. Today, it's a cornerstone of the neighborhood's music scene, with regular acts that include self-proclaimed "hillbilly band" Roe Family Singers and the KFAI House Party Presents series.

The bar is also known for other events, including trivia nights and a drunk spelling bee. On the second Sunday of every month, 331 is also home to Dr. Sketchy's Anti-Art School. A cross between a life drawing class and a Vegas cabaret, this international movement is a two-hour drawing session where the models include burlesque dancers, drag performers, fetish artists, and circus artists. While that might sound like a schtick on steroids, it's actually an earnest enterprise where anyone from an MCAD student to a retiree in search of a hobby spends an afternoon working on their drawing skills. It's fun and supportive – most participants can draw, but you won't go into a shame spiral if you can only manage stick figures – and a great way to be reminded that creativity is here for the taking.

If you're hungry, you can order off the homestyle menu of The Sheridan Room, 311's casual sibling restaurant next door. Try the Big Ass Chicken Cordon Boom sandwich.

Address 331 13th Avenue Northeast, Minneapolis, MN 55413, +1 (612)331-1746, www.331club.com | Getting there Bus 824 to Broadway Street Northeast and University Avenue or bus 11, 32 to 2nd Street and 13th Avenue Northeast | Hours Daily noon–2am | Tip After you're done sketching, head over to Elsie's and bowl a few frames (729 Marshall Street Northeast, Minneapolis, MN 55413, www.elsies.com).

2 35W Bridge Remembrance Garden

A somber memorial to lives lost

If you lived in the Twin Cities on August 1, 2007, chances are your phone lit up sometime after 6:05pm with anxious calls and texts from loved ones, checking to make sure you weren't on the Interstate 35W bridge when it collapsed into the Mississippi River. Tragically, for the families and friends of the 13 people who died and the 145 who were injured, there was no reassuring news on the other end of the line.

That disaster brought international attention to the challenges facing our nation's aging infrastructure. An investigation by the National Transportation Safety Board found that the 40-year-old bridge, which was the third busiest in the state, had a design flaw that couldn't withstand the weight added to the bridge over the years, such as when concrete structures were installed to separate lanes.

A 10-lane replacement was quickly rebuilt, opening just over a year later. The new model is equipped with the latest sensor technology to monitor any strain on the structure. It is also adorned with decorative blue lighting that, when seen from a distance, makes the bridge look like it's floating above the river. The colors change for important events too. When Prince died, the purple streaks of light on the bridge looked almost like streams of tears.

To honor the victims of the collapse, the city erected the 35W Bridge Remembrance Garden. Located on West River Road next to Gold Medal Park, the memorial includes a black granite wall with the names of the 171 total survivors. It's a somber backdrop for the 13 I-beams that stretch 81 feet (a tribute to the date 8/1 or August 1) that are inscribed with the names of the deceased. At night, the beams glow with the same blue light that's on the bridge, which can be seen in the distance. There are also biographies of the victims, ensuring that future visitors don't forget them.

Address West River Road, Minneapolis, MN 55415, across from Gold Medal Park, www.35wbridge.org | Getting there Bus 7, 22 to Washington and 11th Avenues South | Hours Unrestricted | Tip Continue your contemplation across the street with a visit to the beautiful and interactive sculptures and installations at Gold Medal Park (2nd Street and 11th Avenue South, Minneapolis, MN 55415, www.goldmedalpark.org).

3__6th Avenue SE Gateway

Historic Marcy-Holmes in miniature

Thanks to the boom in glass-skinned apartments that line the Mississippi River, it's hard to believe that the community we now call Marcy-Holmes is the oldest neighborhood in Minneapolis. Once its own town, which went by the name of St. Anthony Falls, Marcy-Holmes was incorporated into the city in 1872. The stories of its early days tell of a time when industrious young men with names like Pillsbury saw that the power generated by St. Anthony Falls could fuel their flour mills, not to mention their fortunes.

With so many historic homes and buildings stretching from East Hennepin and Central Avenue to the University of Minnesota's Dinkytown, Marcy-Holmes makes for one of the city's top walking tours. The best place to start is on 6th Avenue SE, between 4th Street SE and Main Street. Known as the Marcy-Holmes Gateway, these two blocks connect the community to the river and the Stone Arch Bridge. They also function as open-air gallery, with 24 miniature bronze recreations of the neighborhood's most historically significant buildings and homes, including the Pillsbury A Mill, once the world's largest flour mill, on Main Street; the Woodbury Fisk home, an 1870 Italianate Revival at 424 5th Street SE; and the university's landmark Dinkydome, which started its life as the Minnesota Bible College.

Created by local artist Aldo Moroni, who was known for his fanciful depictions of historic architecture and urban life, the statues can be used as a three-dimensional atlas to alert you to the neighborhood highlights (only a handful are no longer standing). Each statue includes a plaque telling you the address as well as a few important details. For deeper insights, the Marcy-Holmes Neighborhood Association website offers links to several self-guided tours, including "Hiding in Plain Sight," an audio tour based on the book by the same name by local historian Penny Petersen.

Address 6th Avenue Southeast between 4th Street Southeast and Main Street, Minneapolis, MN 55414, www.marcy-holmes.org | Getting there Bus 6 to University and 6th Avenues Southeast or 4th Street and 6th Avenue Southeast | Hours Unrestricted | Tip Walk across the Stone Arch Bridge to 212 11th Avenue South, the building that housed Minneapolis' last-surviving bordello, which is included in Penny Petersen's most recent book *Minneapolis Madams: The Lost History of Prostitution on the Riverfront*.

4 American Swedish Institute
A castle of culture

From the looks of this turreted mega-mansion on Park Avenue, you'd be tempted to think this museum and cultural center focuses a purely romantic gaze on all things Scandinavian. But step inside, and you'll discover an institution that asks complicated questions about contemporary life. Exhibits range from Swedish photographer Magnus Wennman's poignant-to-the-point-of-haunting portraits of children who have fled Syria to memorial hair jewelry, death masks, and other cultural artifacts of mourning from the museum's permanent collection.

Once the home of newspaperman Swan Turnblad, who was the owner and publisher of *Svenska Amerikanska Posten*, the largest Swedish-language newspaper in the US, the "castle," as it was called, was built in the early 1900s and was clearly designed to telegraph Turnblad's wealth to the rest of the city. The Turnblad family lived there for 21 years before donating it to the organization that would become the American Swedish Institute.

It's a gorgeous historic home, rich in carved wooden balustrades and fireplace mantles and authentic Swedish tile stoves. If you want to see the house at its best, visit during the run up to Christmas, when it's decked out for Yule traditions and events, like children's choirs with girls wearing white dresses and Santa Lucia crowns. You may also experience the celebration of the *tomte*, the sometimes naughty gnomes who are associated with the winter solstice and holiday season.

A new modern addition houses a gallery, gift shop, and Fika, a popular and critically acclaimed café that's named for the Swedish tradition of taking a daily break to drink coffee, eat sweets, and connect with friends and family. The menu moves well beyond desserts to open-faced sandwiches, gravlax, and, of course, meatballs. A creative cocktail menu and Minnesota-made aquavit round out the offerings. Skål!

Address 2600 Park Avenue, Minneapolis, MN 55407, +1 (612)871-4907, www.asimn.org | Getting there Bus 27 to 26th Street East and Park Avenue or bus 39 to Portland Avenue South and 26th Street Southeast | Hours Tue & Thu – Sat 10am – 5pm, Wed 10am – 8pm, Sun noon – 5pm | Tip On 3rd Avenue South, take in a play at the renowned Children's Theatre Company (2400 3rd Avenue South, Minneapolis, MN 55404, www.childrenstheatre.org), which specializes in turning beloved children's stories into shows for the entire family to enjoy.

5 Architectural Antiques

Mingle with the ghosts of buildings past

When St. Joseph's Hospital in St. Paul underwent an extensive renovation and expansion, the original medical library wasn't included in the upgrade. Designed in 1916, the wood-paneled room wasn't built until 1924, after World War I was over. With all that history, not to mention beamed ceilings and bookshelves encased in leaded glass, it was a treasure the hospital didn't want to see chopped up and tossed in a dumpster.

So they called Architectural Antiques, a massive (25,000-square-feet) history museum / oddity warehouse / hardware store extraordinaire in Northeast Minneapolis that's been saving and selling all manner of architectural jewels for over 40 years. The store not only agreed to salvage the library's parts, it reassembled them so that visitors could experience the room almost as it was when it was built.

The staff at Architectural Antiques are passionate about their wares, whether it's a chandelier from the original Milwaukee Auditorium, a bishop's chair or confessional from a decommissioned church, or a cast brass coat hook. They can talk to you about the heraldry images in Tudor revival homes and the history of 1950s school chairs. At Architectural Antiques, every sale comes with an extensive backstory.

The store's bread and butter is lighting, and there's plenty of it, from mission sconces with green slag, to waterfall crystal chandeliers, to simple porch lights. And the selection of "house jewelry" – better known as hardware – is delightfully overwhelming. If you don't have the patience to sort through baskets of doorknobs and pocket door pulls and antique toilet paper holders, just ask for help. These guys will help you find the perfect bronze hinge or decorative lock and key set. Truly, no request is too arcane. When a couple wanted to make their Hong Kong bed and breakfast feel like a castle, Architectural Antiques, half a world way, was their go-to resource.

Address 1330 Quincy Street Northeast, Minneapolis, MN 55413, +1 (612)332-8344, www.archantiques.com | Getting there Bus 10 to Central and 14th Avenues Northeast or bus 17 to Broadway and Monroe Streets Northeast | Hours Mon–Sat 10am–5pm | Tip Continue your architectural salvage tour with a stop and a refresher at nearby Tattersall Distilling (1620 Central Avenue Northeast, Suite 5, Minneapolis, MN 55413, www.tattersalldistilling.com), a distillery and cocktail room that's decorated with a crystal chandelier and fireplace mantle from Architectural Antiques.

6_Art with a Point

Tattoo you and Prince too

When Awen Briem was a kid, he got into trouble at school for drawing on his homework, his shoes, his hands. Any surface that could hold ink, Briem was covering it with doodles and sketches. As he got older, Briem knew he wanted to be an artist, so he tried photography, where he made a living shooting weddings and real estate listings.

Then, in his words, "dumb luck" struck the day he got his first tattoo on his 21st birthday. "This is something I can get down with," he thought. Tattoos, he realized are not like a T-shirt decal, where you order up a style and *voilá*, it appears on your bicep. "People get tattoos at a time when they need a bookmark," he explains. "Almost without exception, they are a rite of passage." His oldest first-time client was 86. She'd always wanted a tattoo, but her husband didn't approve. When he died, she contacted Briem.

That combination of collaborative artistry and stewardship appealed to Briem. So he changed course and got a gig as a shop assistant at Tatus by Koré, a tattoo studio near Uptown Minneapolis. In 2001, he opened his own studio, Art With A Point.

Briem is known for Celtic and geometric designs and his collaborative, one-of-a-kind artistic process. After an initial consultation, customers wait months for an appointment, a period that reflects both Briem's popularity as a tattoo artist and his belief that an expression that's so personal (and permanent) shouldn't be an impulse buy.

He waives that wait, however, for tourists who are visiting the Twin Cities to visit Paisley Park and other Prince landmarks. As a superfan himself, Briem understands that other superfans experience more emotional resonance by getting their Prince tattoos near Uptown. "They want a physical, tangible connection," he explains, while "I Want To Be Your Lover" plays in the background in his sun-filled studio above Lake Street. "I just can't say no."

Address 711 West Lake Street, Suite 511, Minneapolis, MN 55408, +1 (612)823-1254, www.artwithapoint.com | Getting there Bus 21, 53 to Lake and Lyndale | Hours By appointment | Tip See designs of a different kind, or even take a class, at Highpoint Center for Printmaking (912 West Lake Street, Minneapolis, MN 55408, www.highpointprintmaking.org).

7__Ax-Man Surplus

Sorry, the iron lung is not for sale

Sure, this surplus store on University Avenue in St. Paul might be the perfect place to go if, say, you have a project in mind that calls for a banana plug, an electric motor, a roll of duct tape, and a computer fan. But probably the best way to experience this dusty tangle of gas masks, wig heads, beakers, old VCRs, and miles and miles of hardware and gadgets is probably just to go and let inspiration strike. Who knows what kind of mismatched masterpiece could spring from welding goggles, a pack of dice, a garden hose repair kit, and adhesive fake sideburns?

Billing itself as a destination for "artists, tinkerers, engineers, makers, and freaks and geeks of all styles," Ax-Man specializes in scientific, industrial, electronic, and mechanical surplus as well as arts and crafts supplies and "failed consumer products." The company has three Twin Cities outposts and a website where you can buy stuff online, but the St. Paul store is so delightfully creepy – thanks in part to the working iron lung that rests like a coffin amongst the merchandise – that you owe yourself a visit. There are other surprises, too, including a mannequin wearing Santa hightops – bet you didn't know those were a thing – sitting crossed-legged in a partially opened closet and an almost life-size bobblehead Jesus, which sadly is not for sale.

Ax-Man refreshes its stock daily, and the products are mostly new. It's the perfect source for that fourth grade diorama project or costume party or workbench session. The staff exude the brand of oddball humor you'd expect from a place that's known for its quirky hand-drawn signs, some of which look like a collage you'd hang in your locker if you graduated from high school in 1979. One reads: "Sponges for when you have to clean the lizard tank…(If you know what we mean)." Not sure we do, but if the Ax-Man team recommends it, you know it's worth a look.

Address 1639 University Avenue West, St. Paul, MN 55104, +1 (651)646-8653, www.ax-man.com | Getting there Metro to Snelling Avenue (Green Line) or bus 16 to University Avenue and Fry Street | Hours Mon–Fri 9am–7pm, Sat 9am–6pm, Sun noon–5pm | Tip Continue your foraging a few blocks away at Midway Used & Rare Books, which boasts "an eclectic mix of over 100,000 books, comics, magazine, and pulps" (1579 University Avenue, St. Paul, MN 55104, www.midwaybook.com).

8 Bauhaus Brew Labs

Work, play, and drink award-winning beer

When musician-turned-lawyer Matt Schwandt talked his wife and in-laws into opening a family-run brewery, they knew they needed to bring something completely unique to the Twin Cities craft beer scene. That something was making updated lagers, a type of beer that's fermented with a species of yeast that requires lower temperatures to work its magic. The result is a crisper, lighter beer along the lines of a Czech pilsner or, closer to home, the more traditional offerings of the August Schell Brewery in New Ulm.

That the Bauhaus Brew Labs team has succeeded wildly – their Wonderstuff Neü Bohemian Pilsner won a bronze medal at the 2016 World Beer Cup – is a testament to the creative spirit that, like the Bauhaus School philosophy of art and design, promotes the idea that work, play, and life should be joyfully intertwined.

That spirit of discovery starts when you drive down Tyler Street in Northeast Minneapolis. A small sign points you through what appears to be an alley. But hold on: you'll soon discover you've landed in a secret world that's been hiding behind the industrial façade of the former Crown Iron Works, the same company that provided the steel for many of the cities' skyways and the IDS Crystal Court in downtown Minneapolis.

With soaring ceilings and natural light that seems to have been permanently switched to bright, the Bauhaus brewery, tap room, and beer garden that opens the moment the thermometer hits 60F degrees, are so jolly and colorful that you could almost imagine them as the perfect place to host a child's birthday party. Since that's not possible, act like a kid yourself by playing a game of corn hole or bingo. Then eat a grilled cheese from one of the food trucks parked by the beer garden. In the summer, there's even a Night Market featuring local makers in the courtyard. At Bauhaus Brew Labs, youthful enthusiasm is what's on tap.

Address 1315 Tyler Street NE, Minneapolis, MN 55413, +1 (612)276-6911,
www.bauhausbrewlabs.com | Getting there Bus 10 to Central and 14th Avenues Northeast |
Hours Wed & Thu 4–11pm, Fri 3–11pm, Sat noon–11pm | Tip If you're a fan of modern
furniture, discover the discounted finds at the BluDot Outlet, just a few doors up from
the brewery (1323 Tyler Street Northeast, Minneapolis, MN 55413, www.bludot.com/
minneapolis-outlet).

9 Bell Museum Dioramas

Where taxidermy comes alive

Founded in 1872 by the Minnesota Legislature, the Bell is the state's natural history museum. Held in trust by the University of Minnesota, the extensive collection and exhibits endured for decades in a cramped and run-down art deco building on the U's main campus.

Everything changed in 2018, when a new, 92,000-square-foot museum opened on the edge of the St. Paul Campus. The $79 million building has a state-of-the-art planetarium, an observation deck, and a green roof. It is landscaped with native plants. There is much to do here, from holding 10,000-year-old fossils – the Bell was the first natural history museum in the country to allow visitors to handle items from its collections – to observing honeybee hives, to guided stargazing events.

The museum is most famous for its world-class dioramas, which depict Minnesota wildlife scenes, such as gray wolves exploring a Lake Superior shoreline and beavers building a dam on Lake Itasca. While the taxidermy is certainly impressive, the diorama backgrounds are works of art in and of themselves. They were painted in the 1940s by Minnesota native Francis Lee Jaques, who worked as an artist at the American Museum of Natural History in New York City. Each is a masterwork, often depicting treasured locations in the gentle glow of a late afternoon light.

Transporting the dioramas into their new home was no easy task. Workers were required to cut holes through the old building and then haul the works across the river on flatbeds. Many of the displays hadn't been cleaned since they were originally installed. Dust and sediment had dulled nature's colors (not to mention the furs' natural sheen). So museum workers performed some gentle repair work, including fluffing up birds' plumage and washing and regluing leaves. The results are dazzling and vivid depictions of our state's exquisite natural heritage.

NORTH
WOODS
GARDEN

Address 2088 Larpenteur Avenue West, St. Paul, MN 55113, +1 (612) 626-9660, www.bellmuseum.umn.edu | Getting there Bus 61 to Larpenteur Avenue and Coffman Street; the free UMN St. Paul Circulator also makes regular stops at the Bell's main entrance | Hours Tue–Sun 10am–5pm | Tip Check out the U's impressive collection of fashion and textiles at the nearby Goldstein Museum of Design (1985 Buford Avenue, 364 McNeal Hall, St. Paul, MN 55108, www.goldstein.design.umn.edu).

10 Betty Danger's Country Club

Where the 99% hangs out

From the minute you step foot in this Northeast Arts District hotspot, it's abundantly clear that this "country club for the other 99%" isn't going to offer a driving range, bridge tables, or paddle tennis. Yes, the place is awash in as much hot pink and lime green as a Lilly Pulitzer store, but the servers are more likely to sport septum rings and neck tattoos than ribbon headbands and signet rings.

The story is that Leslie Bock, the owner of Psycho Suzi's Motor Lodge and the uptown tattoo shop St. Sabrina's Parlor in Purgatory, decided to take up golf but was dinged when she applied for membership at a local country club. So she turned the sting of social rejection into her next business idea. Located on the Mississippi just across the Lowry Avenue Bridge, Bock's restaurant and bar feels more like a demented playhouse than a clubhouse, complete with a mini-golf course accessorized with a plaid cow, an oversized gorilla, and an apple you can sit inside. (To be honest, it might be a strawberry.) Betty Danger's Country Club is a full-on gimmick. But it's also a hoot.

The highlight is The Danger, a ferris wheel with open-air cars that can seat at least four people. You're allowed – frankly, you're encouraged – to bring your booze (the drinks are on the strong side) and appetizers (Tex-Mex is the house cuisine) with you for the twenty-minute ride, which rotates s-lo-w-l-y above the trees to reveal views of downtown Minneapolis and the industrial northern edge of the city's riverfront. Blankets and warm drinks are provided in the winter, but dress appropriately so as not to tempt the frostbite fates.

Kids are welcome – it's a country club after all – but will probably feel more comfortable during the day, before the scene on The Danger starts to feel like rush week at a fraternity–which, Lord knows, could be the inspiration for Bock's next zany business.

Address 2501 Marshall Street Northeast, Minneapolis, MN 55418, +1 (612)315-4997, www.bettydangers.com | Getting there Bus 32 to Lowry Avenue and Marshall Street Northeast or bus 11 to Lowry Avenue and Grand Street Northeast | Hours Check website for seasonal hours | Tip Continue the kooky fun at Betty Danger's sister bar and restaurant, Psycho Suzi's Motor Lodge (1900 Marshall Street Northeast, Minneapolis, MN 55418, www.psychosuzis.com). It's a modern tiki bar with a bad attitude. (And by bad, think good, with a tiny umbrella on top.)

11 Bob Dylan Mural
Tangled up in all kinds of colors

Pretty much every self-respecting Minnesotan knows that when Bob Dylan graduated from Hibbing High School on the Iron Range, he headed to the Twin Cities. And there is no shortage of pilgrimage stops where you can honor this homegrown legend. There's the former Gray's Drugstore building (now LRx Loring & Pharmacy Bar) in Dinkytown, where Dylan lived in a second-floor apartment by the alley. And there's also Orfield Labs, which used to be Sound 80 studio, where Dylan and some Minnesota musicians re-recorded half of his "Blood on the Tracks" album in December 1974.

And who could forget his performance at Northrop Auditorium at the University of Minnesota, where he played on November 4, 2008, the night Barack Obama was elected president. That night, he announced to the crowd, "I was born in 1941. That was the year they bombed Pearl Harbor. I've been living in darkness ever since. It looks like things are going to change now."

In 2015, Minneapolis formalized our devotion to Dylan with a five-story mural on the corner of 5th Street and Hennepin in Minneapolis, just down the street from the Orpheum Theater, which Dylan used to own. The work was commissioned by the building's current owner, Goldman Sachs, in 2015 as part of Hennepin Theatre Trust's efforts to help revitalize downtown Minneapolis with a Cultural District. Brazilian artist Eduardo Kobra's *The Times They Are A-Changing* is a triptych that depicts three different stages of Dylan's artistic life, from the young folk singer to the white-hatted elder statesman. The portraits are almost photorealistic, except that they're layered with Kobra's distinctive harlequin patterns that are so vibrant they stop just short of being psychedelic. It's a flash of color on a corner that – especially in winter – had suffered from a bad case of the blahs. Today, it's one of the most popular spots in town, especially for taking selfies.

Address The corner of Hennepin Avenue and 5th Street North, Minneapolis, MN 55402 | Getting there Metro to Warehouse/Hennepin Avenue (Green & Blue Line) or bus 4,6 to Hennepin Avenue and 5th Street North | Hours Unrestricted | Tip Five blocks away on Washington Avenue, savor the coffee and crepes at Penny's, a coffee shop (100 South Washington Avenue, Main Lobby, Minneapolis, MN 55401, www.pennyscoffee.com) in the light-soaked 41-foot-high lobby designed by Minoru Yamasaki, who designed the original World Trade Center twin towers in New York.

12 Cafesjian's Carousel
A ride with history

In 1988, word leaked to the local media that Philadelphia Toboggan Company 33 (PTC 33), better known as the Minnesota State Fair's carousel, was to be sold at auction. This news came as a huge shock to fans of the historic ride, who had wrongly assumed their adored 1914 merry-go-round was owned by the fair and therefore would remain in place for as long as its 68 horses could leap to the songs of the Wurlitzer 153 band organ.

A St. Paul couple, Peter Boehm and Nancy Peterson, learned they could purchase PTC 33 for $1.1 million. So they sprang into action and started a media blitz, announcing they had created a non-profit organization, Our Fair Carousel, Inc., that would work with the city to keep the carousel in Minnesota. The donations poured in – from children sending in spare change to a $600,000 gift from a mystery donor who was later revealed to be Gerald L. Cafesjian, an executive at West Publishing Company. Boehm and Peterson traveled to New York and completed the purchase 10 minutes after the auction had started.

PTC 33 moved from the fairgrounds and, after an unsuccessful stint in downtown St. Paul's Town Square, Our Fair Carousel was able to raise enough money to build a new pavilion is St. Paul's Como Park, where it has operated May–October since 2000.

Not only is the carousel a touchstone for many Minnesotans – one woman has had her photo taken annually on the "Alligator Horse" (named for the carving on its saddle) since she was 3 years old – it's a masterpiece of artisanship. Each horse is hand-carved with surprising emotion. You could spend an afternoon analyzing their different expressions and saddle markings (the lead horse has a crest that says PTC). The Carmel horse, located on the outside row, was carved by acclaimed carver Charles Carmel in the famous Coney Island style. You can spot it by its fish scale saddle blanket and dog head at the cantle.

Address 1225 Estabrook Drive, St. Paul, MN 55103, +1 (651)487-8201, www.ourfaircarousel.org | Getting there Bus 3, 83 to Como Avenue and Beulah Lane or bus 83 to Hamline Avenue and Midway Parkway | Hours Please check website for opening hours. | Tip Lose yourself in the flora and fauna at the indoor gardens at the Como Park Zoo & Conservatory (1225 Estabrook Drive, St. Paul, MN 55103, www.comozooconservatory.org).

13__Can Can Wonderland

A mash-up of mini golf and spiked ice cream

Imagine Willy Wonka's chocolate factory as if it were designed by Dr. Seuss, and you'll start to get the feel of the madcap creativity afoot at this indoor arcade and maker space. Housed in a former canning factory in St. Paul's Hamline-Midway neighborhood, Can Can Wonderland is an indoor boardwalk, complete with a wall of vintage pinball machines, foosball tables, and other test-your-luck games from decades gone by. It's also Minnesota's first arts-based public benefit corporation.

To that end, there are art installations, performances, and an impromptu maker workshop where you can try your hand at creating whatever you want with the materials available. Kids and adults working together can fabricate amazing things, transforming piles of cardboard into dinosaurs, helmets, or even a Spanish galleon.

The centerpiece of the whole shebang, however, is an artist-designed mini-golf course, where each hole was created by a different team. There's a twirling cloth tornado, a light-up miniature ferris wheel, and a blue frog that digests golf balls, which roll up his tongue and plop onto the turf through his rear end. Gramma's Living Room is a hole with crocheted afghans, framed cross-stitched slogans, and even an upsetting clown portrait. More holes are in the works, and if you peek behind the massive blue tarp in the hallway outside the entrance, you can get a preview of coming attractions.

Mindful of the fact that it's a business and needs to turn a profit, Can Can has two bars and a concession stand with a carny-inspired menu that tips its hat to the hipster clientele with *bahn mi* hot dogs and "Irish" nachos that come with beer cheese sauce, green onions, peppers, and sour cream. The alcohol selection is dizzying, and includes plenty of spiked ice cream drinks, including the Aye Aye Captain, which is a malt laced with bourbon, Cap'n Crunch, and sprinkles.

Address 755 Prior Avenue North, Suite 004, St. Paul, MN 55104, +1 (651)925-2261, www.cancanwonderland.com | Getting there Metro to Fairview Avenue (Green Line) or bus 67 to Fairview Avenue North and Minnehaha Avenue | Hours Thu 11am–11pm, Fri 11am–midnight, Sat 10am–midnight, Sun 10am–10pm, over 21s only after 9pm | Tip Across the hall, the St. Paul Tool Library (755 Prior Avenue North, St. Paul, MN 55104, www.mntoolibrary.org) lends out anything from table saws to post-hole diggers to sewing machines so that you actually park your car in your garage rather than use it for storing your tools and equipment.

14_ Caspian
Persian cuisine and more

Hossein Azhakh arrived in Minnesota from Iran in 1979, at the peak of the Iranian Revolution. After finishing college at Mankato State University, he decided he wanted to try his hand at the food industry. In 1986, he convinced his two brothers to join him in starting Caspian, a Persian bistro and international food market on University Avenue. The brothers chose the neighborhood because Persians prize education above all else, and they felt that the close proximity to the University of Minnesota would put their business in an area where people were more open to and appreciative of people and cuisines from new cultures.

The Azhakhs thinking proved to be an inspired business decision. More than 30 years later, Caspian is the elder statesman on this constantly evolving street – when they opened there was no TCF Stadium or light rail – that links Minneapolis and St. Paul. The Azhakh family has never advertised the store or the restaurant, and judging by even the weeknight dinner crowds, it's not a strategy they need to second-guess. The restaurant serves what Hossein Azhakh likes to think of as "food of life," from *zeytoon parvardeh*, a paste of green olives and walnuts that's aged with pomegranate puree, garlic, and spices, to grape leaves, to seasoned tenderloin skewers.

The market has an almost overwhelming selection of bulk nuts: almonds, pistachios, hazelnuts, mixed nuts, and also what Azhakh insists are the freshest walnuts in the metro – ask for a taste and you'll likely agree. They also specialize in Middle Eastern flat breads, including pocket bread, *Barbaree* (recommended by the Queen of England, apparently), *lavash*, and *sangak*. There are loads of other delicacies, such as olives, dates, figs, dried cherries, honey balls, and a gourmet Turkish delight. If you are trying a recipe from this part of the world, or just want a delicious meal, Caspian Bistro and Gourmet Marketplace is your Twin Cities resource.

Address 2418 University Avenue Southeast, Minneapolis, MN 55418, +1 (612)623-1113 |
Getting there Metro to Stadium Village (Green Line) or bus 6 to University and
25th Avenues Southeast | Hours Tue–Thu 11am–8:30pm, Fri 11am–9pm, Sat noon–9pm,
Sun noon–8:30pm | Tip Caspian doesn't serve alcohol. If that's an issue, meet up for a pre-
drink at Stub & Herbs on Oak Street (227 Southeast Oak Street, Minneapolis, MN 55455,
www.stubandherbsbar.com).

15_ CC Club

An iconic dive bar

It's Monday at 2:30pm, and the regulars, many of whom have already drained their first round of Jack and Cokes, don't seem in any rush to give up their seats at the bar. "Nel blu dipinto di blu," known to most of us as "Volare," is on the jukebox, and Dean Martin's voice serenades a room that's as dark as ink, save for the Christmas tree lights strung across the ceiling and the collection of vintage beer signs that shine against the wood paneling. They cast a flattering light on a booth of women friends who are throwing a few back.

Welcome to the CC Club, Minneapolis's most storied dive bar. Opened on the heels of Prohibition as the CC Tap, today it's famous for being the favorite beer-and-booze joint for many of the musicians who have defined the Minneapolis music scene over the years. The Replacements, Soul Asylum, Curtiss A, The Suburbs, and Twin/Tone Records co-founder (and manager of the late great Oarfolkjokepus record store) Peter Jespersen, this bar was their second home. Word is that The Replacements' Paul Westerberg wrote "Here Comes a Regular" about the CC. Comedian Tom Arnold lived across the street before he married Roseanne Barr. A drink in one hand without a cigarette in the other was a significant shift in the lives of the bar's long-time clientele.

Business took a hit when smoking was banned in bars across the state. And CC Club loyalists were sent into a tizzy in 2013, when French Meadow, the "healthy" organic restaurant next door that's known for its earnest clientele and menu items such as a micro-greens and kale salad called the "Zen," bought the bar. But the new owners insisted they had no interest in changing a classic. So if you spend an evening at the CC, you'll still get to play decades worth of hits on their jukebox. And even though the food is better than it was during its seedier heyday, take heart: you can order 5 different varieties of Heggies famous pizza to go with your pitchers of Grain Belt.

Address 2600 Lyndale Avenue South, Minneapolis, MN 55408, +1 (612)874-7226, www.ccclubbar.com | Getting there Bus 4, 113 to Lyndale Avenue South and 26th Street West | Hours Mon–Thu 11am–2am, Fri & Sat 8am–2am, Sun 10am–2am | Tip If you want to try that salad, the French Meadow Bakery & Cafe (2610 Lyndale Avenue South, Minneapolis, MN 55408, www.frenchmeadowcafe.com) is right next door. Their menu is fabulous and features a beautiful array of farm-to-table plates and rich desserts.

16__ The Cedar Cultural Center
Intercultural appreciation through music

The Cedar, as it's affectionately known, is the only all-ages music venue in the Midwest. That means parents can up their cool factor by taking their skeptical teenagers to see Amadou & Mariam or Rickie Lee Jones. And it also means that they won't risk seeming like losers because they can't keep their eyes open past midnight. At this former 1948 movie theater in Minneapolis' Cedar Riverside neighborhood, every show is over before curfew.

Born out of the American folk music revival that took hold in coffeehouses across the United States in the 1950s and 1960s, The Cedar is the place in the Twin Cities to see folk legends like Greg Brown, whose shows sell out year after year. It's also known for its extensive roster of international artists. If you want to understand Korean percussion, dig into the nuances of accordion playing in Cape Verde, discover a little-known singer-songwriter, or enjoy night club music from Mogadishu in a theater that's located in the neighborhood with the largest Somali diaspora in the United States, this beautifully time-worn theater is your place.

Located in a former 1948 movie theater, the main room has a sprung hardwood floor, which made it the perfect venue when, in its early days after it was founded in 1989, The Cedar was also known as the place to learn zydeco and the Carolina shag. The theater still boasts a strong dance tradition, but it's more known for music today. The room is intimate—you're never more than 30 feet from the stage.

With an extensive network of volunteers who run concessions and help set up chairs in exchange for free tickets, The Cedar cares deeply about being a good neighbor. Since 2014, it's partnered with Augsburg College to create the Midnimo program (*midnimo* means "unity" in Somali), which offers residencies for Somali musicians from across the world as a way to promote understanding of Somali Muslim culture through music.

Address 416 Cedar Avenue South, Minneapolis, MN 55454, +1 (612)338-2674, www.thecedar.org | **Getting there** Metro to West Bank (Green Line) or bus 22 to Cedar Avenue and Riverside Plaza | **Hours** See website for performance schedule | **Tip** Have a pre-show dinner at Afro Deli & Grill (720 Washington Avenue Southeast, Minneapolis, MN 55454, www.afrodeli.com). Try the Afro Steak Dinner and wash it down with Somali sweet spiced tea.

17 __ Chicago Avenue Fire Arts Center

Where sparks fly

The closing of the streetcar line in the early 1950s was a devastating blow to the four neighborhoods that share the corner of Chicago Avenue and 38th Street in Minneapolis. Residents lost their transportation, and the Nokomis Theater, which opened in 1915 to show silent movies, was shuttered. The area fell on hard times.

In 2009, as part of a neighborhood renewal initiative, six residents broke ground on a plan to turn the Nokomis Theater into the Chicago Avenue Fire Arts Center (CAFAC), a place where people can practice any creative process that involves heat, spark, or flame. It's a discipline that can include blacksmithing, welding, fabricating neon signs and glass beads, and repoussé, an ancient art where you create intricate, raised designs that are hammered into the back of a piece of metal. You can also learn "fire performance," the art of dancing and juggling with flaming objects.

What might seem like a narrow niche turned out to be an inspired plan for both neighborhood revitalization and the needs of local artisans. "You can't do this in your basement," says Heather Doyle, CAFAC's artistic director, referring to the expensive equipment, not to mention the insurance issues associated with operating torches, furnaces, and hot metals.

Today, CAFAC is a busy place where people in safety goggles pound against anvils and pour molten metal into molds. At night, you can literally see sparks fly and forges glowing through the windows. And if you're not ready to make – much less use – your own set of flaming nunchucks, don't sweat it. The center hosts all manner of demonstrations, gallery shows, and artist talks. It also offers what they call the SPEAK project, a summer program where kids ages 5 to 18 create public art for their communities.

Address 3749 Chicago Avenue South, Minneapolis, MN 55407, +1 (612)294-0400, www.cafac.org | Getting there Bus 5, 23 to Chicago Avenue South and 38th Street East | Hours Gallery, Sat 10am–3pm; see website for class schedules and events | Tip Check out *Hothouse Mural*, located on CAFAC's exterior north wall (3749 Chicago Avenue South, Minneapolis, MN 55407, www.artsonchicago.org/hothouse-mural), which illustrates the actual goings on inside the building.

18 Commodore Bar & Restaurant

Toss 'em back at one of F. Scott's haunts

The Grand Commodore Hotel opened in St. Paul's Cathedral Hill neighborhood in 1920, at a time when Cathedral Hill was booming – the recent construction of the St. Paul Cathedral would define the area. It was the time of the Jazz Age, Harlem Renaissance, women's emancipation. And it was the era of Prohibition and bathtub gin. Home to both F. Scott Fitzgerald – who apparently spent plenty of time in the basement speakeasy – and Sinclair Lewis, The Commodore was also known as a swanky place wealthy families moved to when the Depression forced them out of their Summit Avenue mansions.

When Prohibition was lifted, The Commodore took on a new life, aided largely by a knockout art deco bar, created by acclaimed Berlin set designer Werner Wittkamp, who also was the visionary for Ziegfeld Follies' stages. As the economy recovered, this glamorous hangout took off, and was even the occasional watering hole for gangsters Ma Barker and John Dillinger.

Then, in 1978, a gas explosion decimated everything but the bar. Thankfully for all of us, this historic space has recently benefited from a Hollywood-level facelift. Decorated in black and white with touches of gold, it shimmers not only in the light cast by chandeliers, but also the glow of bottles shining through the two backlit bars. The effect is so elegant you'll wish you'd swapped out that down vest for a dinner jacket and had brushed up on the Charleston.

The menu draws from the age of the Harlem Renaissance too, while retaining its modern authenticity by updating standards that include lobster deviled eggs, buttered sole, and a wedge salad. The Fitzgerald cocktail honors the author's supposed preference for gin (the story goes that he thought people couldn't smell it on his breath) and is a luscious glass of liquid gold.

Address 79 Western Avenue North, St. Paul, MN 55102, +1 (651)330-5999, www.thecommodorebar.com | **Getting there** Bus 21 to Selby and Western Avenues or Selby Avenue and Arundel Street | **Hours** Tue–Sat 4pm–midnight | **Tip** Walk to 599 Summit Avenue, St. Paul, MN 55102, which is the brownstone where Fitzgerald wrote *This Side of Paradise*.

19 Como-Harriet Streetcar Line

Clang, clang, clang goes the trolley

At its peak in the 1920s, the Twin Cities Rapid Transit (TCRT) operated over 500 miles of streetcar line, which stretched from Stillwater and Bayport on the metro's east side, to Excelsior, Deephaven, and Tonka Bay on the west. TCRT even had steamboats for passengers to transfer to when they arrived at Lake Minnetonka.

Then, in 1949, a group of outside investors took control of the organization and focused on busses, which were less expensive to maintain. So began the downfall of one of the country's top public transportation systems. By 1954, the streetcars were gone – sold to other transit systems, including Newark, New Jersey and Mexico City. San Francisco still owns a few, which you can ride on the Market Street Railway.

Today, the streetcar line exists only as a phantom limb – many of our bus lines travel the same routes, although most of us don't know it. One exception is the mile of the original line between Lakewood Cemetery on Bde Maka Ska and the Linden Hills Station across from the Lake Harriet Bandshell in Minneapolis. Operated by the Minnesota Streetcar Museum, the Como-Harriet Streetcar Line runs from May through October. On a summer evening when the sun is reflecting off the lakes, it's a serene ride past the cemetery and the archery fields, through a below-street-level pass into "Cottage City," which is what Linden Hills was called back when it was a summer retreat for the Minneapolitans who lived downtown.

The Minnesota Streetcar Museum operates four trolleys on this line, including No. 1300, which was built in 1908 at TCRT's Snelling Shops in St. Paul, and No. 322, which was built in 1949 to be fancy enough to compete with automobiles. We know how that story ended, but this living museum celebrates when the car was definitely not king.

Address The Linden Hills Depot and Museum is located at 4200 Queen Avenue South, Minneapolis, MN 55410, www.trolleyride.org | **Getting there** Bus 6 to Upton Avenue South and 43rd Street West | **Hours** Check the website for details | **Tip** Lake Harriet is a bonanza of activities. Start by walking east to Lyndale Park's Rose Garden and Peace (Rock) Garden (4124 Roseway Road, Minneapolis, MN 55409, www.minneapolisparks.org).

20_ The Cowles Center

Devoted to dance

When it opened in 1910, the Sam S. Shubert Theatre on 7th Street North in downtown Minneapolis was one of 60 palatial playhouses built by the New York-based Shubert Theatrical Company, whose network included the Sam S. Shubert Theatre in St. Paul, now the Fitzgerald Theater (see ch. 40), and several legendary Broadway theaters, including the Winter Garden and the Imperial.

When the area surrounding the Shubert, now referred to as Block E, devolved into a collection of flophouses, seedy bars, and head shops, the city council voted to raze the Beaux Arts jewel. Thus began a decade-long battle to save the theater, which ended happily when preservationists got the Shubert added to the National Register of Historic Places.

With the Shubert's future assured, Artspace, a nonprofit that is a national leader for developing properties that benefit artistic communities, recommended transporting the building to Hennepin Avenue, where the 5.8-million-pound building could get a new life next door to the Hennepin Center for the Arts. It was the heaviest building ever to be moved on rubber tires and took 12 days to travel the two blocks to its new location.

Today, the Schubert has been renamed the Goodale Theater. It is the largest performing space in The Cowles Center for Dance & the Performing Arts, which is the metro's flagship institution for dance. The headquarters of some of the area's top dance companies, including the Minnesota Dance Theatre, James Sewell Ballet, and Zenon Dance Company, it's also home base for the Illusion Theater and Twin Cities Gay Men's Chorus. If you're in the mood for something a little more experiential, the Cowles Center offers a mind-boggling menu of classes: flamenco, break dancing, classical northern Indian dance, and more. If you want to learn the mamba or a dance from the African diaspora, this is your place.

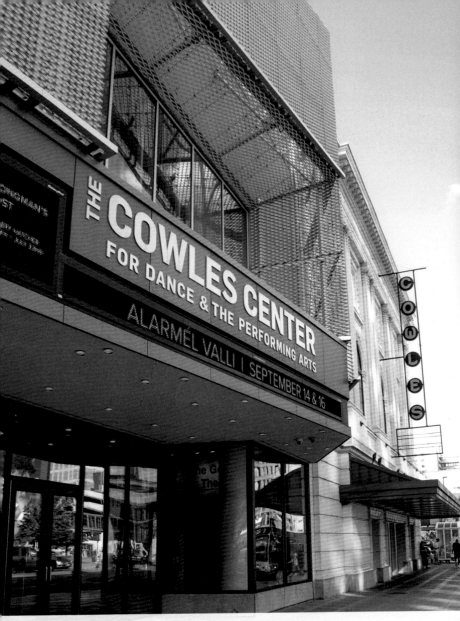

Address 528 Hennepin Avenue, Minneapolis, MN 55403, +1 (612)206-3636, www.thecowlescenter.org | Getting there Metro to Warehouse Hennepin Avenue (Blue & Green Line) or bus 4, 6, 10, 11, 12, 17, 18, 25, 59, 61 to Hennepin Avenue and 5th Street/6th Street North | Hours See website for performance schedules | Tip Before a performance, have an old-school dinner at Murray's, a classic steakhouse that's been in business since 1946 (26 South 6th Street, Minneapolis, MN 55402, www.murraysrestaurant.com).

21 Crosby Farm Regional Park

Hike to a hidden slot canyon

In 1858, English immigrants Thomas and Emma Crosby purchased 160 acres on the Mississippi River near what is now Shepard Road and 35E, where they raised chickens, cows, and pigs, and farmed potatoes and apples. One of the largest farms in the area, it changed hands several times until 1962, when it became a public park. Today, Crosby Farm Regional Park, part of the Mississippi National River and Recreation Area, is one of the only places in the Twin Cities to take amble through floodplain forests that open up to views of oak-lined bluffs.

Crosby Farm is a great place to spot wildlife, especially where the park connects with Hidden Falls Park at the confluence of the Mississippi and Minnesota Rivers. This is a bird highway, especially during the fall and spring migrations. You'll spot wood thrushes, Nashville warblers, catbirds, chipping swallows, indigo buntings, and scarlet tanagers. If you're lucky, you'll see a red-tailed hawk coasting on an updraft or, toward evening, hear the hoots of a great horned owl. Bald eagles, turkey vultures, and great blue herons also call this green pocket of St. Paul home.

If you are feeling adventurous, there is even a secret slot canyon, which isn't marked on the trail maps. This spot is particularly popular in winter for ice climbing, thanks to a frozen waterfall – but please don't start scaling the wall unless you are with someone who has experience! To get to this little-known gem, walk east toward Crosby Lake, then take the narrow trail that edges the bluff. Keep going a few hundred feet, hike into the creek bed (don't worry, it's usually dry), and into the canyon. Voila!

Afterward, wind down on almost seven miles of hiking trails, which you can snowshoe during winter. Or pack a picnic and enjoy the views on one of the secluded river beach walks.

Address 2595 Crosby Farm Road, St. Paul, MN 55116, +1 (651) 293-0200, www.nps.gov/miss/planyourvisit/crosfarm.htm | Getting there Bus 82 to Davern Street/Norfolk Avenue and Shepard Road | Hours Daily dawn–9pm | Tip Use the bike trail to get to Lilydale Regional Park, another wild place on the edge of the city (950 Lilydale Road, St. Paul, MN 55118, www.nps.gov/miss/planyourvisit/lilydale_park.htm).

22__Czech and Slovak Protective Society Hall

Exercise with history

Founded in 1862 in Prague, the Sokol movement is an all-ages gymnastics and calisthenics practice and philosophy that was created in part as an egalitarian way to express national pride when the Czech lands (now the Czech Republic and Slovakia) were ruled by the Hapsburg dynasty. Promoting physical, intellectual, and moral training, this "sound mind in a sound body" spirit is alive today in towns across the world with Czech and Slovak communities.

In the Twin Cities, you can experience Sokol at the Czech-Slovak Protective Society (CSPS) just off West 7th Street in St. Paul. The CSPS was originally a fraternal order that provided insurance to community members who were coping with a death or other disasters, and their building is the oldest in the country that was founded by Czechs and Slovaks and is still used by their descendants. Built in 1887, it's also the oldest ethnic community hall in Minnesota.

CSPS hosts its share of weddings, funerals, and potluck celebrations. It's also home to Czech and Slovak Sokol Minnesota, which has a timeworn yet still beautiful theater/gymnasium on the hall's second story and calisthenics classes for all ages. Participants often travel to Iowa to take place in an annual *slet*, a mass gathering where hundreds to thousands of people do calisthenics routines set to music(the word means "gathering of birds," which is a reference to the fact that *sokol* means "falcon").

CSPS also hosts community classes, from folk dancing to dumpling making. Whatever activity brings you there, history will assert itself, whether it's the portraits of long-dead members on the third floor or the peepholes that were used to enforce the members-only policy. There is also a theater that has gorgeous backdrops that were painted in the 1920s.

Address 383 West Michigan Street, St. Paul, MN 55102, www.sokolmn.org | Getting there Bus 70, 74 to 7th Street West and Superior Street | Hours Vary according to class times. | Tip After going through some hard times, the historic residential streets around West 7th Street have been spiffed up and make for a lovely walk, especially by the Mississippi. Then head up the hill to the flagship store of heritage leather goods maker J.W. Hulme (867 Grand Avenue, St. Paul, MN 55105, www.jwhulme.com).

23 Dairy and Meat Salesroom

Foodstuffs from the classroom

Driving past the crop fields and barns on University of Minnesota's St. Paul Campus is a reminder that even in a time when most of our state's population lives in cities, we also have a proud commitment to our agricultural roots, even if it's just shopping at a downtown farmers' market or dining at a farm-to-table restaurant serving duck chorizo *enmoladas* or pickled garlic scapes.

There's another, mostly unknown, opportunity to buy hyper-local products at the university's Andrew Boss Laboratory of Meat Science. That's where every Wednesday afternoon the staff at the Meat and Dairy Salesroom stock the freezers, switch on the fluorescent lights, and let the public buy the meat, cheese, ice cream, and honey that food science students have made during research projects and in classes such as "Livestock and Carcass Evaluation" and "Pork Production."

It's a popular event that draws customers from off campus, which is the point because our food scientists have a lot to brag about. Since the early 1900s the University has been nationally known for its dairy product research, including procedures for making blue cheese, which researchers originally aged in caves on the Mississippi. Try the Nuword, an extremely sharp blue cheese that was invented here using a white strain of bacteria, which means it's white, even though it's officially labeled blue. A milder version is available in a spread. There are also some unique ice cream options, including Minnesota Sundae, which is vanilla mixed with honey and sunflower seeds.

Across the room in the meat locker, you can find anything from cottage bacon, which is cut from the shoulder instead of the belly and comes in a shape of a disk instead of strips (making it better for sandwiches, apparently) to rump roasts, to racks of spare ribs, to ox tail. You can also get suet for your birdfeeder if your birds are hungry.

Address Room 166, 1354 Eckles Avenue, St. Paul, MN 55108, +1 (612)624-7776, fscn.cfans.umn.edu/research-services/dairy-salesroom | Getting there Bus 87 to Cleveland and Carter Avenues North or bus 124 to Eckles and Carter Avenues | Hours Wed 2–5pm | Tip The Good Acre, a food hub that connects regional farms with local communities, sells CSA shares for the freshest local produce.

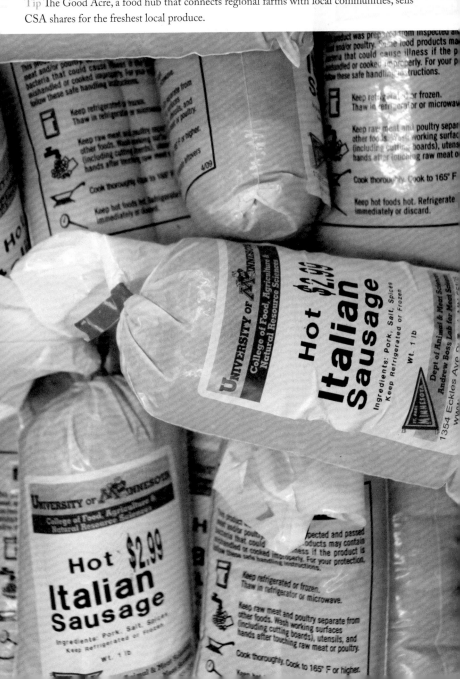

24 District del Sol

South of the border to the North

People of Mexican heritage started moving to St. Paul's West Side Flats neighborhood around the time of World War I. The community was small until the 1980s, when there was an upswing in immigration from Mexico and other Central American countries. Today, if you drive down Wabasha Street from downtown St. Paul, you'll notice not only that the road changes its name to Cesar Chavez Street, but that the gray storefronts are replaced by ochre, burnt umber, and orange. This is the District del Sol, a thriving collection of Latino-owned restaurants, businesses and community centers.

The vibrant neighborhood is anchored by two family-owned businesses that act as the district's bookends: Boca Chica and El Burrito Mercado. Boca Chica (www.bocachicarestaurant.com) has been serving up marinated cactus and *mole poblano con pollo* since 1964. In addition to being a taste of home for the neighborhood, Boca Chica offers a taste of home for the neighborhood, and it was the first taste of Mexican food that rose above the Minnesota-based (and non-spicey) Chi Chi's or the Taco Bell precursor Zantigo for local *gringos*.

Almost a half-mile away on Cesar Chavez Street, El Burrito Mercado (elburritomercado.com) has been run by the Silva family since 1979. Tom and Maria Silva moved here from Aquascalientes, Mexico and started a business selling Mexican dry goods and tortillas. Today their daughters and granddaughter are in charge of the 13,000-square-foot market, which now includes a grocery store with a meat department, deli, and shelves stocked with products from Goya, La Costeña, and La Preferida. There's also an authentic Mexican bakery, where you can gorge on *tres leches* cake and conchas, and a cafeteria – try the *gorditas* – as well as a sit-down restaurant and bar.

Mrs. Silva still travels to Mexico to meet with the artisans who make anything from serapes to Day of the Dead *retablos*. You can also buy traditional star piñatas and the goodies that go inside them.

Address Cesar Chavez Street, St. Paul, MN 55107 | Getting there Bus 68, 71 to Cesar Chavez and State Streets | Hours Unrestricted | Tip More than any other neighborhood in St. Paul, District del Sol is known for its street murals, which you can marvel at on foot or from your car.

25 Dred and Harriet Scott
The history of enslaved people at Fort Snelling

Located on Bdote, a Dakota homeland, Fort Snelling is perhaps the most well-known historic site in Minnesota. But what's not as widely acknowledged is that by the time the fort was built in the 1820s, there were slave owners in the Northwest Territory, even though slavery was prohibited. The Minnesota Historical Society, which owns and operates Fort Snelling, estimates that during this period, between 15 and 30 enslaved people worked at the fort at any given time. In fact, Colonel Josiah Snelling, the fort's first commander, was a slave owner.

In the 1830s, African American Dred Scott was taken by Army surgeon John Emerson, the man who owned him, to Fort Snelling, where he met an enslaved woman named Harriet Robinson. Dred and Harriet were married at the fort. When Emerson was reassigned to the South, they moved with him.

But when Emerson died, his widow wouldn't allow Scott to buy freedom for himself or his family. The Scotts filed a lawsuit for their freedom in the Missouri state court system, claiming that their residence at Fort Snelling, technically a free territory, automatically freed them. Their fight went to the US Supreme Court in 1857. The court ruled that African Americans were not citizens and therefore had no right to sue in federal court. The ruling outraged abolitionists and was a precipitating factor in the Civil War. The Scotts were freed by a subsequent slave owner in 1857.

Today, you can tour Fort Snelling, including what was probably Dred and Harriet Scott's home, a single room on the lower level of the reconstructed hospital building. The Historical Society isn't sure exactly where the Scotts lived, but they chose this location because it would have been in close proximity to Dr. Emerson's quarters. Docents here share information about the Scotts, their lives at the fort, their lawsuit for freedom, and lessons that still resonate today.

Address 200 Tower Avenue, Minneapolis, MN 55111, +1 (612) 726-1171, www.mnhs.org/fortsnelling | Getting there Bus 7F to the turnaround closest to the fort | Hours See website for seasonal hours | Tip Pay your respects to those who have served in the armed forces at Fort Snelling National Cemetery, a beautiful and solemn green space near the airport. University of Minnesota hockey legend John Mariucci is buried in Section R, Site 1569 (7601 34th Avenue South, Minneapolis, MN 55450, www.cem.va.gov/cems/nchp/ftsnelling.asp).

26__Electric Fetus

Browse the stacks at Prince's favorite record shop

So what if *National Lampoon* once singled out the Electric Fetus for having the worst business name possible? This Minneapolis record shop, which opened in 1968, is so beloved that Prince – Prince! – was spotted buying CDs there five days before he died. Ringo Starr even wore a Fetus T-shirt to the Grammys.

The Fetus got its start on the West Bank of the University of Minnesota, which at the time was the heart of the Twin Cities' hippie scene. The counterculture was in full swing, and one of the owners was given a citation for refusing to take down a poster that showed John Lennon and Yoko Ono's "Two Virgins" album cover – the one where both go full frontal – superimposed with Pat and Richard Nixon's faces.

The store moved to its current location in 1974. Today, it feels much like it did back then: floors the color of butterscotch that are worn smooth from all the foot traffic; the smell of sandalwood incense; a killer sound system where you hear every top note and downbeat; heads bent over the rows of vinyl, even in the middle of the day.

What's more, the staff are approachable and eager to help but don't lord their encyclopedic musical knowledge over you. So if you need a gift for your nephew, you won't feel embarrassed that you have zero appreciation for emo or indie pop. Near the cashier, a white board lists the live shows in town – the Fetus also sells tickets. And there are frequent in-store performances by both local and national bands.

But the main event is the library's wealth of new and used vinyl and CDs. In the mood for a mint condition copy of "The Best of Buffy Sainte-Marie," Parliament's "Mothership Connection," or Chuck Mangione's "Feels so Good"? Chances are they're here in the nerve center of the Twin Cities music scene. And if you can't find that perfect Little River Band album, head over to the novelties section and snag a rubber unicorn mask.

Address 2000 4th Avenue South, Minneapolis, MN 55404, www.electricfetus.com, +1 (612)870-9300 | Getting there Bus 2 to Franklin Avenue East and 4th Avenue South or bus 39 to Portland Avenue South and Franklin Avenue East | Hours Mon–Fri 9am–9pm, Sat 9am–8pm, Sun 11am–6pm | Tip Stick with the cultural theme and head over to 3rd Avenue to check out the masterpieces at the Minneapolis Institute of Art (2400 3rd Avenue South, Minneapolis, MN 55404, www.artsmia.org).

27 __ The Elf Tree

He believes in you

Each Minneapolis lake has its own crowd. Tucked into the city's southern edge, Lake Harriet is *the* place for families, many of whom bring their strollers and tagalong bikes from the nearby kid mecca of Linden Hills to feed the ducks, practice rollerblading, or enjoy a picnic at the Lake Harriet Bandshell.

Harriet's child-friendly ethos is perhaps mostly fully on display at the lake's southern shore, where if you look carefully you'll notice a tiny wooden door in the base of an ash tree on the walking path. No, it's not the home of the Keebler dudes baking their Fudge Shoppe cookies. It's the summer residence of Mr. Little Guy, an elf who for twenty years has been answering the hundreds of letters that are left at his doorstep between Memorial Day and Labor Day.

The ritual goes something like this: someone, usually a very young child, writes a note to Mr. Little Guy, perhaps asking him questions about his life or confiding wishes or secrets. Occasionally the person will leave a trinket, a piece of candy, or a drawing. Within a few days, a typed note addressed to that very penpal appears behind the same door. Each is a sweet and earnest reminder of the generosity and goodwill that pulses through this busy city.

Mr. Little Guy is extremely media-averse, and because he's tiny enough to walk through a door that's smaller than a box of cake mix, he has managed to remain unseen for over two decades. But this much we know: according to the *Star Tribune*, which has published many accounts, Mr. Little Guy likes to eat minnow pies and bake chocolate chip cookies. He says he gets some of his best jokes from ladybugs. His bicycle is the size of a mushroom.

Most of all, Mr. Little Guy is a touching reminder that everyday acts of kindness really do matter. One of his favorite sign-offs is, "I believe in you." And because the always-generous Mr. Little Guy believes in us, we most definitely believe in him.

Address Lake Harriet Parkway at South Queen Avenue, Minneapolis, MN 55409 | Getting there Bus 6 to 44th Street West and Upton Avenue South or bus 46 to 50th Street West and Queen Avenue South | Tip Keep the magic going with a visit to Linden Hills and the Wild Rumpus, one of the country's preeminent independent children's bookstores (2720 West 43rd Street, Minneapolis, MN 55410, www.wildrumpusbooks.com).

28__Eloise Butler Wildflower Garden and Bird Sanctuary

A walk in the woods

Opened in 1907, this native plant garden is the oldest of its kind in the United States. It's less than five minutes by car from the center of downtown, but when you walk through its gate you feel like you have stumbled into the Frances Hodgson Burnette's original *Secret Garden*. The park is named for Eloise Butler, a retired botany teacher, who not only petitioned the park board to create the garden, but also served as its curator until she died at age 81, while on her way to work. Her ashes were spread in this patch of leafy beauty she so lovingly helped create.

While the garden is closed during the winter, every other season has something special to offer. The woodland areas bloom every April and May with trillium, bluebells, and trout lilies. June and July are the best months for wetland species, including lady's slippers – the Minnesota state flower – and native irises. Sunflowers and asters burst on the scene in mid to late summer, while the fall is a showstopper for prairie grasses and autumn foliage.

There's even a cabin, the Martha Crone Visitors Shelter, which serves as an interpreter center, with hands-on natural history displays (skulls, nests, feathers, you get the idea), an excellent selection of reference books, and very knowledgeable volunteers. Named for Butler's assistant, who succeeded her as the garden's curator, it's as cozy and secluded – and as much of an unexpected surprise – as something you'd find in a fairy tale, but with no scary overtones. On cold days, you can even warm up next to the fireplace.

Home to over 500 plant species, Eloise Butler is also perfect for an afternoon of bird watching. From downy woodpeckers, to fox sparrows, to evening grosbeaks, over 130 species of birds announce their presence with their whistles, chirrs, tuks, and yeeps.

Address 1 Theodore Wirth Parkway, Minneapolis, MN 55405, +1 (612)370-4903, www.minneapolisparks.org | Getting there Bus 9 to Wayzata Boulevard North and Wirth Parkway | Hours Apr 1–Oct 15 daily 7:30am–one hour before sunset; Oct 15–Mar 31 weekends only | Tip Extend your time in nature by crossing Theodore Wirth Parkway to walk in the Quaking Bog (Theodore Wirth Parkway and Glenwood Avenue, Minneapolis, MN 55411, www.naturefind.com/places/quaking-bog), a highly unusual ecosystem and a wonderful place for spotting shimmery dragonflies.

29__The Endless Bridge

Cocktails at stage left

Since 2006, the acclaimed Guthrie Theater has called a navy blue citadel, that looks like it was delivered by a spaceship, home. Designed by French architect Jean Nouvel to make the most of its setting on the Mississippi River, the building became an instant landmark that's now the queen of the revitalized Mill District in downtown Minneapolis. But while most Twin Citians can spot it, many aren't aware that you don't need a ticket to one of the Guthrie's plays to explore the building's public lobbies, including the Amber Box, which is wrapped in yellow windows, creating the effect of a sunny day, even when you're in the depths of March gloom. Nouvel got the idea for the window tint while he was wearing ski goggles, and the experience can cast a new light on the worst of moods. If you are afraid of heights, however, stay away from the window in the Amber Box's floor because it opens up to a vertigo – inducing view of the street nine floors below Yikes.

Downstairs, the cantilevered lobby known as the Endless Bridge is one of the best places in town to enjoy a glass of wine, especially when the weather is nice and you can stand outside on steps that are steep enough to make you feel like you could trip and end up in the froth of St. Anthony Falls. Stretching more than half a block from the building's face, the 30-foot-wide cantilever sticks out from the theater like a thumb that's trying to hitch a ride – some have likened it to a gangplank. The physics will freak you out if you dwell on them, but are thrilling nonetheless.

Inside, the windows on the bridge walls are all set on predetermined sightlines and are lined with mirrors to give a focus to the views, including some of historical landmarks, such as the Washburn A Mill and Gold Medal Park. They are yet another reminder that, when framed correctly, all the world's a stage. (And while you're there, ask at the box office about last minute theater tickets.)

Address 818 South 2nd Street, Minneapolis, MN 55415, www.guthrietheater.org, +1 (612)377-2224 | Getting there Metro to US Bank Stadium (Green & Blue Line) or bus 7, 22 to Washington and Chicago Avenues South | Hours Mon 8am–8pm, Tue–Sun 8am–11pm on performance days and 8am–8pm on non-performance days | Tip From May through October the Mill City Farmers Market sets up shop on the Guthrie's plaza (704 South 2nd Street, Minneapolis, MN 55415, www.millcityfarmersmarket.org).

30 _ Firefighters Hall & Museum

A hot time in the old town

In 1985, Minneapolis Fire Department Captain Bill Daniels and his wife Bonnie established a trust fund to benefit retired firefighters. They hoped their funds could be used one day to establish a community space where former firefighters could connect with each other, and a museum that would educate the public about the history of firefighting and the importance of fire safety and prevention.

Since 2004, the fruits of the Daniels' generosity have had a home in the Holland neighborhood, near Edison High School in Northeast Minneapolis. That's where the Firefighters Hall & Museum is housed in a 12,500-square-foot former manufacturing plant that was overhauled to showcase and preserve the museum's extensive collection of engines, pumpers, ladders, alarms, and protective gear. As you can imagine, the museum does a great birthday party business for the under-seven crowd, but you'll enjoy it even if your college graduation is a distant memory.

The museum is much more than an homage to the mechanics of firefighting, although if that interests you, you'll be satisfied. It also celebrates our city's largely unknown relationship to firefighting. There's the smoke extractor that was invented by the Minneapolis Fire Department's repair shop in 1926, paving the way for the exhaust fans that now suck smoke and gases from burning buildings. And there's the state's first fire alarm telegraph system, which came to St. Paul in 1873 after 300 citizens signed a petition for a way for the public to summon the fire department in an emergency.

Perhaps the most moving exhibit for today's visitors is *81 MINUTES: After the Bridge Collapsed*, which details the role firefighters and first responders played after the I-35W Bridge collapsed. It's an emotional reminder of how everyday heroes willingly work in harm's way.

Address 664 22nd Avenue Northeast, Minneapolis, MN 55418, +1 (612)623-3817, www.firehallmuseum.org | Getting there Bus 17 to Washington Street and 22nd Avenue Northeast or bus 32 to 22 Avenue Northeast and Edison High School | Hours Sat 9am–4pm and by appointment on weekends | Tip If you are so inspired, stock up on heavy duty work clothes and flame-retardant apparel at Minnesota Glove & Safety (203 Marie Avenue East, West St. Paul, MN 55118, www.minnesotaglove.com).

31 Food Building

A rising enterprise

Kieran Folliard knows his way around the food and beverage business. When the Irish-born founder of Kieran's Irish Pub, The Local, The Liffey, and Cooper Pub sold his eateries in 2011, he launched 2 GINGERS Whiskey, a company he named after his red-headed mother and aunt. When Beam Suntory bought that company just a year later, pretty much everyone in town knew that Folliard wasn't going to retire.

When he's not traveling the country evangelizing for 2 GINGERS, Folliard is a guiding force behind Food Building, an incubator of artisan food entrepreneurship at its most creative and fun. Housed in a 26,000-square-foot repurposed industrial space in Northeast Minneapolis, Food Building is part maker space, part gathering spot, part public classroom. If you like the behind-the-scene glimpses into food production at the State Fair, you'll enjoy watching the action taking place behind Food Building's massive plate-glass windows.

Food Building has three anchor tenants: Red Table Meat Co., Baker's Field Flour & Bread, and Alemar Cheese Company. At Red Table, you'll see pigs sliced straight down the middle and hanging from one hoof, the blood draining out of their insides and onto the floor. Founder Mike Phillips buys whole pigs from small, sustainable Minnesota farms that practice humane slaughter to create his artisan line of pork products, including speck, coppa, and pancetta.

The scene at Baker's Field is a bit less dramatic, but no less fascinating. Founded by Steve Horton, the visionary behind Rustica Bakery, who saw a need for fresh-milled flour, it's the first new flour mill in the metro in decades as extremely strict laws to prevent flour explosions have been a disincentive (see ch. 66). The delicious fruits of these three Minnesota makers can be enjoyed at Kieran's Kitchen Northeast, Folliard's cozy Food Building restaurant, bar, and market (117 14th Avenue NE, Minneapolis, www.kieranskitchen.com).

Address 1401 Marshall Street Northeast, Minneapolis, MN 55413, +1 (612)545-5555, www.foodbuilding.com | Getting there Bus 30 to Broadway and Marshall Streets Northeast or bus 11 to 2nd Street and 13th Avenue Northeast | Hours Self-guided tours are Tue–Fri 10am–5pm (production is most active in the morning). Call to arrange private tours/tastings. | Tip Check out the edible trees and plants at the Bancroft Meridian Garden Food Forest, the first food forest in Minneapolis (38th Street and 12th Avenue, Minneapolis, MN 55407, www.facebook.com/bancroftneighborhood).

32 Foshay Observation Deck
The best view in town

When it opened in 1929, the 32-story Foshay Tower was the tallest building in Minnesota and the first skyscraper to be built west of the Mississippi River. It remained the tallest building in Minneapolis for 48 years until 1972, when the glassy Philip Johnson-designed IDS tower soared into the sky, making the Foshay look like an elf standing next to Santa.

Designed to pay homage to the Washington Monument, the Foshay was the brainchild of utilities magnate Wilbur Foshay. Locals clucked that it was too flashy – and with the letters FOSHAY printed on all four sides of the building – too self-aggrandizing for the modest Midwest. Those naysayers certainly didn't shut up when, for the building's grand opening, Foshay commissioned John Phillips Sousa to write a special march to commemorate the event.

Unfortunately for Foshay, the stock market crash happened two months after the building opened. He was over-leveraged, to the point where even the $20,000 check he wrote to Sousa bounced. That was the beginning of a downward spiral that hit bottom when Foshay was convicted of mail fraud and sent to Leavenworth Penitentiary. (He was later pardoned by President Truman.)

Despite that ignoble start, the tower that bears Foshay's name is perhaps the loveliest example of art deco architecture in downtown Minneapolis. Now a W Hotel, it also has the only outdoor observation deck in the city. Wrapping around the entire 31st floor, it no longer offers uninterrupted views – you're only waist high to some of the buildings surrounding it – but that's actually even more fun because you get a visceral feeling of the scale of buildings you are used to seeing from street level. You'll also be struck how the Twin Cities is so flat you can practically see to Wisconsin. Inside, there's an interesting museum that tells the history of the building and Minneapolis during the time it was built.

Address 821 South Marquette Avenue, Minneapolis, MN 55402, +1 (612)215-3783,
www.wminneapolishotel.com/foshaymuseum | Getting there Bus 22, 19, and 5E to
8th Street and Marquette Avenue/2nd Avenue South | Hours Thu–Mon 11am–5pm |
Tip On the Foshay's street level, have brunch at Keys, a breakfast and brunch eatery
for classic American comfort food (114 South 9th Street, Minneapolis, MN 55402,
www.keysfoshay.com).

33 Frankenstein's Monster Exhibit

Get shocked at the Bakken Museum

"Electricity is a subject where one meets the marvelous at every turn." That quote from 18th-century French scientist Charles François de Cisternay du Fay, which greets you when you enter this Tudor/Gothic mansion, might seem quaint from the perspective of the 21st century, but keep an open mind. While the Bakken Museum *is*devoted to what would seem to be a rather narrow focus on the electrical world, you'll soon discover that those sparks of energy suffuse everything, from a stormy sky to our own bodies.

Electricity also inspired one inventor's imagination. The seed for the Bakken was planted in 1976 when Earl Bakken, the creator of the battery-powered pacemaker and the co-founder of the medical technology company Medtronic, bought West Winds, a mansion on the southwestern edge of Bde Maka Ska. It was built in 1928 by William Goodfellow, a real estate agent (and purported paranoid tightwad). But Bakken never actually lived in the house. He bought it to store his collection of instruments and appliances that documented the history of electricity in the life sciences, as it had outgrown its space at Medtronic's headquarters.

The museum is a monument to Bakken's quirky interests, from Ben Franklin's kite flying – you can crank up an electrostatic generator to make your hair stand on end – to Mary Shelley's 1818 novel *Frankenstein*. Many of Shelley's father's friends were prominent scientists of the day, and the would-be novelist grew up hearing stories about dead frogs' bodies and human corpses shaking when shocked. The Bakken's Frankenstein exhibit is a tribute to Shelley's scary creation story. It includes a recreation of Frankenstein's laboratory, which awakens from its diorama-like dormancy at the touch of a button. But beware. There's a surprise ending that will scare the bejesus out of little kids.

Address 3537 Zenith Avenue South, Minneapolis, MN 55416, +1 (612)926-3878, www.thebakken.org | Getting there Bus 6 to 39th Street West and Zenith Avenue South | Hours Tue–Sun 10am–4pm | Tip When the weather is nice, bring along your swimsuit and beach towel, and head across the street to the southern shore of Bde Maka Ska, where there's a swimming beach and the best sand volleyball courts in town (www.minneapolisparks.org).

34 George Floyd Square
Creative expressions of pain and hope

On May 25, 2020, a 46-year-old Black man named George Floyd bought a pack of cigarettes at Cup Foods, a convenience store in Minneapolis. The store clerk thought Floyd had paid with a counterfeit $20 bill and called the police.

Seventeen minutes after the police arrived, Floyd was unconscious, pinned to the ground by three of the officers, including Derek Chauvin, who pressed his knee into Floyd's neck and kept it there for over eight minutes, even when Floyd told the officers he couldn't breathe. He called out for his mother.

Floyd died on the scene. Videos of the killing became public, and Minneapolis – and the world – erupted in protests decrying what Black Americans had always understood and white Americans had long tried to ignore: Police are over three times more likely to kill Black Americans than white Americans, as confirmed in a 2020 study by the Harvard School of Public Health. Floyd's murder ignited a national reckoning not just about policing in America but also structural racism.

Today, the corner where he died is a place of remembrance and community building, tended to by volunteers, including Jeanelle Austin, the founder of the Racial Agency Initiative. They hope visitors will use their time there to reflect and to support the pain, grief, and hope of the community. Bus shelters have been converted into donation areas for clothing and books.

The space continues to change and evolve. Look for *Icon of a Revolution*, a 12-foot-high, black-and-white mural of Floyd's face. It was created by Peyton Scott Russell, a local artist and founder of Juxtaposition Arts, a teen-staffed arts organization that was the first in town to include graffiti alongside fine arts instruction (www.juxtapositionarts.org). Nearby, on 37th Street, the *Say Their Names Cemetery* art installation honors Black Americans who were killed by the police.

Address East 38th Street and Chicago Avenue, Minneapolis, MN 55407, www.georgefloydglobalmemorial.org | Getting there Bus 14C to Chicago Avenue and 38th Street East, or bus 5E to Portland Avenue and 38th Street East | Hours Unrestricted | Tip After your visit, head over to Pimento Jamaican Kitchen, a Black-owned business that serves delicious jerk chicken, goat curry, and braised oxtail and was also a community safe space during the protests (2524 Nicollet Avenue South, Minneapolis, MN 55404, www.pimentokitchen.com).

35___Glee at the Capri

A must stop on your Prince pilgrimage

In January 1979, a 20-year-old local musician played his first professional show at the Capri Theater on West Broadway on Minneapolis' North Side. Photographer Greg Helgeson was in the fifth row, unknowingly seated near the performer's relatives. Like everyone else in the audience, Helgeson was blown away by the explosive and groundbreaking talent unfolding on the stage.

Helgeson didn't take many photos that night of the legend who would become known across the world as Prince. But one image still hangs in the lobby of the Capri Theater, and it's a heart stopper. Prince is on his knees, his upturned head framed by a massive afro. His eyes are closed, and he seems lost in whatever tune that's pulsing from his heart to his guitar. Taken well before the eccentric purple brocade coats, frilled collars, and high-wasted pants, the portrait is a visual distillation of the frank and beautiful sexuality that is the hallmark of Prince's music.

Built in 1927, the Capri was originally known as the Paradise Theater and was one of 13 movie palaces in North Minneapolis. Today, it's the only one left in the area, and although it hasn't operated as a first-run movie theater for decades, it's been restored and is enjoying a happy new life as a center for the arts. Owned and operated by the Plymouth Christian Youth Center, the theater's programming is a celebration of the many ways that the arts can transform hearts and lives.

You can sing along to the community choirs that are directed by music luminaries Dennis Spears and J. D. Steele, or even show off your stuff at an open-mic night. First Thursday Films is a monthly screening of films – from *Malcom X* to *Beasts of the Southern Wild* – followed by moderated discussions. After falling into disrepair, this beautiful building is, like it was in 1979, a place where people can express themselves and their talents.

Address 2027 West Broadway Avenue, Minneapolis, MN 55411, +1 (612)643-2024, www.thecapritheater.org | Getting there Bus 14 to West Broadway and Logan Avenues or bus 19 to Penn and 23rd Avenues North | Hours See website for event schedule | Tip Head east on West Broadway over the river to The Back Bar at Young Joni. If it's open, you will see a red light framing the door, which is in the alley on the side of the restaurant. Order a Paisley Park cocktail, a yummy combination of pisco, Angostura, violette, ginger, and cassis (165 13th Avenue Northeast, Minneapolis, MN 55413, www.youngjoni.com).

36 Golden Fig Fine Foods
Gourmet goodies

When she was in her early 20s, Wisconsin native Laurie McCann Crowell worked behind the counter at the Barefoot Contessa, a chi-chi specialty food shop founded by the mega-food-celebrity Ina Garten in East Hampton, NY. Thankfully for us all, you can taste Garten's seasonally minded, gourmet influence in the array of products that Crowell makes and then sells in Golden Fig Fine Foods, her beautifully stocked and thoughtfully edited shop on St. Paul's Grand Avenue.

Crowell got her start in the food retail business by making small batches of infused vinegars, and you can buy them here. Try the chocolate balsamic, aged in oak and chestnut barrels, on steak or vanilla ice cream. The apple spice vinegar – actual slices float inside the bottle – is great in coleslaw or a simple green salad. Yucatan balsamic is a fiery combination of ginger, garlic, chile flakes, and habanero that is delicious drizzled over mozzarella. There are also homemade infused sugars – cherry cardamon adds a cozy zing to oatmeal – and the crave-inducing Dilly Pickle Dip. And the dry spice mixes! Try all the unique seasonings, from curries to hot cocoa blends to packets of flavorings for bagel spreads or dips. A smaller selection of Golden Fig products is also available at Lunds & Byerlys.

These products alone would more than justify a store, but the Golden Fig also promotes products by other local companies, including critically acclaimed Sweet Science Ice Cream and Barsy's Almonds (try the "Naughties" almonds flavored with cinnamon, cocoa, and cayenne). But the product that will ruin you for all others is the Stirsby®, a wooden kitchen tool that is a cross between a spatula and spoon, handcrafted from non-first-growth hardwoods and workshop scraps by Edina woodworker John Danicic. Use your Stirsby to mix sauces and risottos, or even to scramble eggs. You will never use a wooden spoon again.

Address 794 Grand Avenue, St. Paul, MN 55105, +1 (651) 602-0144, https://goldenfig.com |
Getting there Bus 21 to Selby Avenue and Avon Street, or bus 63 to Grand Avenue and Grotto
Street | Hours Tue–Sat 11am–6pm, Sun 11am–5pm | Tip Head east on Grand
Avenue to the Grand Hand Gallery, which shows and sells fine American crafts (619 Grand
Avenue, St. Paul, MN 55102, www.thegrandhand.com).

37__Gopher Sports Hall of Fame

The spirit of Ski-U-Mah

In 2000, a shy kid from Hutchinson, MN named Lindsay Whalen made her way to the Twin Cities to attend the University of Minnesota. A high-school basketball star, Whalen arrived at the U without much fanfare, but went on to have such a stellar college career that she became the first Gopher to be drafted into the WNBA. Today, she is a much-adored star of the much-adored Minnesota Lynx.

You can see Whalen's Gophers bobblehead as well as other memorabilia from her college basketball career as the (now-retired) #13 at the T. Denny Sanford Athletics Hall of Fame at the University of Minnesota's TCF Bank Stadium. More than just an homage to the Big 10 football/basketball/hockey juggernaut that gets most of the (good and bad) headlines, the 5,000-square-foot hall is a celebration of what it means to be a college student athlete, a coach, and a fan.

There are trophies galore, of course. But the items that hold your attention and really tell the stories of the college sports experience are definitely more prosaic. On display are baseball coach Dick Seibert's scorebooks from the five seasons when the Gophers went to the College World Series, and the mustard-colored wool leggings worn by wrestlers in 1946. There are the beaten-up cleats used by quarterback Adam Weber, who played 50 consecutive football games during his college career. There are leotards, Speedos, tennis racquets, oars, deflated basketballs and footballs, each accompanied by an explanation that puts it into the greater context of Gopher sports.

And there are megaphones, buttons, maroon and gold letter sweaters, and other mementos of cheerleading and fandom. There's even an explanation of the U's famous "Rah, Rah, Rah For Ski-U-Mah," rouser, which was written in 1884. In case you didn't know, Ski (pronounced sky) is a Sioux battle cry for victory.

Address 420 Southeast 23rd Avenue, Minneapolis, MN 55455 (entrance is between Goldy's Locker Room and the stadium's Ticket Office), www.gophersports.com/trads/hall-fame.html | **Getting there** Metro to Stadium Village (Green Line) or bus 6 to University Avenue and Huron Boulevard | **Hours** Open to all ticket holders on football game days 1.5 hours prior to kickoff, until 30 minutes after the game ends. Admission is free. | **Tip** Start your day with breakfast at campus institution Al's Breakfast (413 14th Avenue Southeast, Minneapolis, MN 55414, www.alsbreakfastmpls.com).

38 Hamline Church Dining Hall

Dishing it out for over 120 years at the State Fair

Sure, the Minnesota State Fair is held for only 12 days every year. But as the largest state fair in the United States in terms of daily attendance (it trails only Texas in terms of total numbers), the Great Minnesota Get-Together is an institution whose devoted fans visit year after year, heading to the same concession stands and attractions over and over again.

For some fairgoers, that annual ritual includes the Hamline Church Dining Hall on Dan Patch Avenue. In operation for over 120 years, it's the longest consecutively run stand in the entire fair and relies on 60 volunteers every day; only the chef and the teenage kitchen workers get paid. In fact, some Hamline Church's volunteers have been recognized by the fair for 50 years of service. They feed the waves of fairgoers who are eager to get a chance to sit down and eat off an actual plate instead of snarfing down novelty foods like Reuben pickle dogs or alligator-on-a-stick.

While the dining hall started out in 1897 by serving homemade sandwiches, at some point – volunteers think it was the 1930s – the church women who ran the place pioneered a new meal to offer in addition to pot roast and baked chicken: the ham loaf. A combination of ground meat and ham that's served with a brown sugar-mustard-vinegar gravy, it has its share of haters. Even so, the dining hall dishes up over 1,000 servings during the fair's run, and it has achieved enough of a cult status that its recipe has appeared in *Saveur*. Regardless of whether or not you want to try this local delicacy, a visit to the dining hall is more than worth it, if only because it's the Fair's only outpost for Izzy's Ice Cream – they create a special flavor every year. Keep your eyes peeled for local celebrities, including Vice President Walter Mondale, whose mother taught Sunday School at the church.

Address 1667 Dan Patch Avenue, Falcon Heights, MN 55113, www.hamlinechurch.org/serve/dining-hall | Getting there Bus 84 to Snelling Avenue and Midway Parkway or bus 3 to Como Avenue and Winston Street | Hours Daily 7am – 7pm, the State Fair is open the last 12 days before and including Labor Day | Tip Do not skip a visit to the Agriculture Horticulture Building (1271 Underwood Street, Falcon Heights, MN 55108, www.mnstatefair.org) to check out the homage to crop-art legend Lillian Colton.

39   Haunting the Fitz
Look for the ghost at stage left

Built in 1910 as part of the nationwide Shubert chain of theaters – its original name was the Sam S. Shubert Theater – the Fitzgerald Theater got its start in part by staging vaudeville productions. In 1933, it changed its name to The World Theater and started showing movies. When a local author named Garrison Keillor brought his show, *A Prairie Home Companion*, to the World in 1981 on public radio stations across the country, he lobbied to have the venue named after St. Paul's most famous literary son. Minnesota Public Radio severed its relationship with Keillor in 2017 over a sexual harassment allegation.

What's not as well known is that the Fitz is haunted. The story goes something like this. During a renovation in 1985, workers taking down a false ceiling found a note addressed to Ben, a stagehand who may or may not have died in the 1940s. That's when things started to get weird. There've been reports of Ben dropping beer bottles to make his presence known. Tools have gone missing and then reappeared in odd places. Empty bottles of Muscatel have shown up where one wouldn't expect to find Muscatel. And Ben's shadow has apparently been spotted sliding across the backstage halls and catwalks. Even creepier, there are stories of a chilled breeze near an entrance that was boarded up long ago.

Staff at the Fitz insist that Ben is harmless, but an accident where a massive chunk of plaster fell and barely missed two employees has given some people pause after the workers who were almost squashed shined their flashlights into the hole left by the plaster and reported seeing a shadowy figure.

Ben isn't alone. Legend has it that he's joined by a second ghost named Veronica, an actress who died at or near the theater. A devoted performer who appreciates The Fitz's stellar acoustics, Veronica likes to practice singing in the theater, where her voice can sometimes be heard throughout the auditorium at night.

Address 10 East Exchange Street, St. Paul, MN 55101, +1 (651)290-1200, fitzgeraldtheater.publicradio.org | Getting there Bus 62, 67, 75, 262 to Wabasha Street and 7th Street | Hours See website for performance schedule | Tip Hamline University (1536 Hewitt Avenue, St. Paul, MN 55104, www.hamline.edu) is especially proud of its haunted buildings, including Old Main, where an apparition was spotted with a noose around its neck.

40_ The Herbivorous Butcher

A must for meatless Monday (or any day)

If you think that a meal without meat means pale cubes of tofu or that protein vegetarians crumble into their chili, you need to head over to Northeast Minneapolis to sample the offerings at The Herbivorous Butcher. This popular niche business – Comedian Jon Stewart is a fan – started as a tiny stand selling "cruelty-free meat and cheese alternatives" at the Minneapolis Farmers Market. Today, it's the country's first vegan butcher shop, offering anything from Cuban pork to Korean ribs to all manner of sandwich meat alternatives, which are displayed in a storefront so minimalist-chic you'd think you were shopping in Copenhagen.

The shop is the brainchild of the sister-and-brother team of Aubry and Kale Walch, who moved here from Guam in 1993 after their father read an article in *Forbes*, which touted Bloomington as the best place in the country to raise kids. During high school, Aubry spent a lot of time in Northeast Minneapolis working as a rave promoter and loved the area's industrial architecture. With the neighborhood's up-and-coming energy, the Walches felt like it was a natural fit for their first store.

Their products are made on the premises. But instead of carcasses and cleavers, The Herbivorous Butcher relies on ingredients such as vital wheat gluten, pinto beans (for heft), and all manner of seasonings and sauces (for flavor and color). It's a surprisingly creative, not to mention artful, enterprise. But given that both Walches are devoted vegans themselves – Aubry has eschewed meat for over 20 years, Kale for five – how can they ensure that their chorizo and dill havarti taste anything like their meat and cheese world inspirations? Their dad, a meat eater, was an early taste tester. Today, he and the entire team of vegan butchers give feedback for new recipes, often relying on their childhood memories of anything from pepperoni to Canadian bacon.

Address 507 1st Avenue Northeast, Minneapolis, MN 55413, +1 (612)208-0992, www.theherbivorousbutcher.com | **Getting there** Bus 4, 61 to 1st Avenue and 5th Street Northeast | **Hours** Tue−Fri 10am−7pm, Sat 10am−6pm, Sun 11am−4pm | **Tip** The rest of the country plays the childhood game Duck, Duck, Goose. But in Minnesota, the kids play Duck, Duck, Grey Duck. We don't really know why this is so, but you can show your Minnesota pride with a "Gray Duck" ski cap from I Like You (501 1st Avenue Northeast, Minneapolis, MN 55413, www.i-like-you-minneapolis.myshopify.com), a gift shop with lots of other gifts for proud Minnesotans.

41 Hindu Society of Minnesota

Visit the standing Vishnu amongst the cornfields

Drive past the strip malls of Maple Grove and toward the housing subdivisions. Keep going until the road narrows and cuts through farmland. The scene is so pastoral that it's hard to remember that you are still in Hennepin County. This sense of disorientation hits a moment of peak confusion when you spot a gargantuan cement structure shooting up from the cornfields. Welcome to the Hindu Society of Minnesota (HSMN), the largest Hindu temple in North America.

Founded in the late 1970s, HSMN started as an informal collection of families who got together in each other's homes to study the *Gita*, conduct worship rituals, and celebrate holy festivals. The first official temple was housed in a decommissioned church in Northeast Minneapolis. As the Minnesota Hindu community grew, so did the need for a larger space. The 80-acre parcel in Maple Grove was purchased in 1998, and the first consecration ceremony at the new, 43,000-square-foot temple took place in the summer of 2006.

The public is welcome to visit whenever the temple is open, and you can also take a guided tour on the weekends. After taking off your shoes, you are led through the building for a 45-minute introduction to the Hindu religion. The moment of awe occurs on the second floor in the Prayer Hall, which is decorated with 21 deities, each in their own shrines. The largest is dedicated to Vishnu, one of the three most important Hindu deities, along with Brahma and Shiva. He is shown standing – HSMN is the first temple in North America to depict Vishnu in this position.

While the façades of Hindu temples in India are decorated with elaborately detailed sculptures, the architects of this temple had to factor in the impact of cold weather on the building's exterior. That's why much of the temple has a streamlined, modern aesthetic.

Address 10530 Troy Lane North, Maple Grove, MN 55311, +1 (833) 469-4766, www.hindutemplemn.org, templetours@hsmn.org | Getting there From 94 West, take exit 213 for County Highway 30 towards Dunkirk Lane North. Turn right onto Lawndale Lane North, left onto 101st Avenue North, and right onto Troy Lane to destination on the right. | Hours Mon–Fri 9:30–11:30am and 5:30–8:30pm, Sat & Sun 9am–8:30pm; tours upon request | Tip Stock up on Indian food staples at India Bazaar in Plymouth (3355 Plymouth Boulevard, Minneapolis, MN 55447, www.indiabazaarmn.com).

42 HmongTown Marketplace
A Southeast Asian street market in Frogtown

An ethnic group with ancient roots in the mountain regions of China, the Hmong have never had a country of their own, although many eventually settled in Thailand and Laos. Because they aided US troops in their fight against Southeast Asian Communists during the Vietnam War, the post-war crackdowns against them were so extreme that many were forced to flee as refugees. Starting in 1975, some resettled in Minnesota. Today, more than 66,000 Hmong call Minnesota home. In fact, the Twin Cities metro has the largest concentration of Hmong in the United States.

A prime gathering spot for this far-flung community is the HmongTown Marketplace on the eastern edge of St. Paul's Frogtown neighborhood. A former lumberyard that was converted into an indoor/outdoor market with more than 200 vendor stalls, this is the place in town to buy anything from papaya salad to *nab vam* – a classic dessert made from jelly, starch bits, chopped fruits, coconut milk, and syrup. You can also find live chickens, martial arts movies, and traditional neon-flecked dresses that are made with more pleats than an accordion.

The produce is an impressive testament to the hard work this resilient community has done to establish farms throughout Minnesota. Thai basil, winter melon, foreign squash, sugar cane, lemongrass, Asian cucumbers – you can get them all here, alongside vendors who support Hmong traditions, including merchants who sell ceremonial burial robes and shoes.

Each year in late November, the community takes over both floors of the mammoth St. Paul RiverCentre to honor Hmong Minnesota New Year, a lively three-day celebration of ancestors, food, and the harvest. Don't miss the *Pov pob*, or "ball toss." It's a courtship ritual, where young men and women toss a small cloth-sewn ball back and forth. Think of it as mass flirting, although some people are hoping to find *the* one.

Address 217 Como Avenue, St. Paul, MN 55103, +1 (651)487-3700, www.hmongtownmarketplace.com | Getting there Metro to Capitol/Rice Street (Green Line) or bus 3 to Como Avenue and Galtier Street | Hours Daily 8am–8pm | Tip Hmong Arts, Books & Crafts is the first and only Hmong bookstore in the world and is dedicated to preserving and celebrating Hmong culture (217 Como Avenue, Suite 108, St. Paul, MN 55103, www.hmongabc.com).

43__Hotel Alma

Minneapolis' most divine urban inn

In 2013, when chef Alex Roberts bought the building that housed his deservedly-worshipped restaurant Alma, he realized that the second floor of the historic building was too beautiful to be wasted on the workaday aesthetics of offices and cubicles. So, in what can only be described as an inspired brand extension, he converted the space into a delightful seven-bedroom inn.

In Europe, many acclaimed restaurants have guestrooms, which can transform a dinner into a memory-making event. That idea struck a chord with Roberts. "We wanted Alma diners to be able to experience that luxury," he says.

And what a luxury it is. Like the restaurant and café downstairs, Hotel Alma is eclectic without being funky, refined without feeling snobby. There's a handmade honesty that is both soothing and sophisticated, from the wooden beds crafted by local woodworker Marvin Freitas, to the cream-colored Moroccan blankets designed by Talin Spring, tastemaker extraordinaire and owner of leather goods company Spring Finn & Co. It's a true getaway for both the heart and soul. And it's the kind of retreat where you could have either the most romantic night of your life or find the headspace to finish your novel. Or both.

Just don't expect the kind of peace and quiet you'd find in the North Woods. "It's an urban inn," admits Roberts. "You'll hear the friendly sounds of the restaurant below and the noises of the street. It's a bustling place that's also very cozy."

That coziness includes the kind of empathetic gestures that transform a hotel into a more soothing version of home: wool slippers, breakfast in bed, and all-natural bath and beauty products that were created by Margo Roberts, Alex's wife. Each scent is so subtly layered – a body mist contains lemon, cedarwood, thyme, grapefruit, and bergamot – that you'll find yourself inhaling just for another whiff, right before your second or third nap.

Address 528 University Avenue Southeast, Minneapolis, MN 55414, +1 (612)379-4909, www.almampls.com | Getting there Bus 6, 250 to University and 6th Avenues Southeast | Hours Lobby access during business hours | Tip If you absolutely must leave Alma Universe, head east on University and take in a performance at Northrop Memorial Auditorium at the University of Minnesota (84 Church Street Southeast, Minneapolis, MN 55455, www.northrop.umn.edu).

44 House of Balls

The funhouse of one man's imagination

"How can you take the material we are surrounded by and value it?" That's the question that drives sculptor Allen Christian to transform the everyday detritus – from clocks to cutlery – that pervades our lives. In 2014, he moved from the North Loop to a 2,800-square-foot building in Cedar Riverside that was previously the home of the underground rock club Medusa. Indeed, a visit to this workspace is a testament to his devotion to creative repurposing.

There are frying pans that, thanks to a plasma cutter, look like portraits of Donald Trump. And there's a robot (or is it Franken-stein?) with arms made from irons. Most of all, there are bowling balls. Christian started carving them years ago, etching away the resin to reveal faces or figures. They soon became his signature, hence the name of his gallery. "At first I thought about calling it Balls to the Wall," he says, "but that was too confrontational."

That Christian would even consider holding back seems a bit odd when you take in the scope of his oeuvre; this definitely isn't the place to go if you are in the mood for watercolor landscapes. His sculptures go just to the edge of creepy, but when Christian describes them, his sincerity and geniality make House of Balls feel more like a carnival than the set of *Game of Thrones*.

House of Balls has been free to the public ever since it opened. And while much of Christian's work is for sale, there are no price tags, which he thinks interfere with the viewer's experience. "There's nothing to sell here except creativity and expression," he says. That's not literally true, of course, but Christian *is* a devotee to the non-commercial philosophies that are a part of public celebrations such as Burning Man. It's a open-hearted generosity that extends to studio visits. While the gallery has set hours, if you drop by when Christian's around, chances are he will invite you in for a tour and a nice long chat even if House of Balls is closed for the day.

Address 1504 South 7th Street, Minneapolis, MN 55454, +1 (612)332-3992, www.houseofballs.com | Getting there Metro to Cedar Riverside (Blue Line) or bus 22 to Cedar Avenue South and 6th Street South | Hours Sat noon–4pm | Tip Now that you're inspired about what to do with those balls, head over the Bryant Lake Bowl for a game or five (810 West Lake Street, Minneapolis, MN 55408, www.bryantlakebowl.com).

45 Hunt & Gather

Vintage amusements from only the best basements

If you think antique stores are filled with either high-back chairs from the days of Betsy Ross or the castoff oil paintings and crocheted afghans from somebody's great aunt's attic, this genre-busting south Minneapolis shop has a surprise for you. Described by *The Wall Street Journal*, as "a seemingly endless series of rooms containing the treasures of a million Midwestern basements," Hunt & Gather has worn the happiest-retail-experience-in-the-metro crown since it opened on Xerxes Avenue in 2003.

The store has 14 vendors, each of whom shares the sensibility of owner Kristi Stratton, who took over the building that used to house American Classics, where she was a vendor. The happy result is a highly edited assemblage of home decor, clothing, and taxidermy that in her words creates "a vintage amusement store." From a collection of Zurah Shriner's convention buttons to primary colored oilcloths to a pair of Ferragamo spectator pumps, Hunt & Gather combines the endless selection of a Central American market with the theatrics and goofball fun of an arcade. A stash of vintage maps and instructional posters – courtesy of Bemidji State University, who sold them when their curriculum and instruction went digital – are so unintentionally chic you'll find yourself thinking you must have a diagram of the epidermis for your living room. Not to mention a wrestling trophy, Mexican serape, or mounted deer's head.

Hunt & Gather is best known for its extensive collection of channel letters, which are the massive custom-made letters that are used on commercial and public buildings. Stratton started collecting them 20 years ago, and now she's the go-to buyer in town when businesses take their signs down. People from all over the metro rent or buy them for weddings and other special occasions when they want make bold proclamations of love or otherwise.

Address 4944 Xerxes Avenue South, Minneapolis, MN 55410, +1 (612)455-0250, www.huntandgatherantiques.com | Getting there Bus 6, 46 to Xerxes Avenue South and 50th Street West | Hours Mon – Sat 10am – 6pm, Sun noon – 6pm | Tip Five blocks south on Xerxes, Pizzeria Lola (5557 Xerxes Avenue South, Minneapolis, MN 55410, www.pizzerialola.com) serves up the most divine artisan pizzas in town. Go during off-peak hours to avoid peak lines.

46 Ingebretsen's

Lingonberries, lefse, and lutefisk, oh my

Scandinavians started immigrating to Minnesota in the late 19th century. In the Twin Cities, many eventually settled in Minneapolis' Longfellow and Cedar Riverside neighborhoods. Just west of Longfellow on the streetcar line, Norwegian American Charles Ingebretsen opened the Model Meat Market on East Lake Street in 1921. Almost a century later, that store, now called Ingebretsen's, expanded down the block and is managed by Charles' granddaughter, Julie, when she took over told her family she'd run the store "for a while." That was in 1974.

Today, Julie still presides over an emporium that includes gifts (Trolls! Waffle irons! Heart-shaped everything!) and a needlework shop where knitters gather to help each other master the intricacies of the *Setesdal* sweater pattern and embroiderers stitch the collars for said sweaters.

The bosom of this Minneapolis landmark is still the old-school butcher shop and deli, where you can buy anything from the signature Swedish meatballs to blood sausages to herring to lutefisk. There's also a well-stocked selection of *lefse*, a traditional Norwegian flatbread, and jars of all kinds of lingonberries, mustards, and syrups.

Just as important as the fact that Ingebretsen's butchers – some of whom have been working behind the counter for 40 years – provide foodstuffs that you can't find anywhere else in town, is the fact that the store is a repository of Scandinavian culture and heritage. At a time when the Norwegians and Swedes have scattered to other parts of the city and the suburbs, Ingebretsen's acts like an informal schoolhouse, where you can learn about all manner of traditions, from *Midtsommer* (the longest day of the year) to *tomte*, the mischievous Swedish sprites who guard farm animals in exchange for a yearly bowl of Christmas porridge. And if you're searching for a Scandinavian bridal crown, this is your place.

Address 1601 East Lake Street, Minneapolis, MN 55407, +1 (612)729-9333, www.ingebretsens.com | Getting there Bus 21, 14 to East Lake Street and Bloomington Avenue South | Hours Mon–Fri 9am–5:30pm, Sat 9am–5pm | Tip Go full Scandihoovian and finish your day with a 6-minute drive on Franklin Avenue to Norway House, an education center dedicated to what's happening in contemporary Norway (913 East Franklin Avenue, Minneapolis, MN 55404, www.norwayhouse.org).

47 __ In the Heart of the Beast Puppet and Mask Theater

Street theater for the soul

Housed in a 1937 art deco movie theater that, by the 1960s, had fallen on such hard times it was screening pornography, In the Heart of the Beast Puppet and Mask Theater (HOBT) combines the ancient arts of puppetry and mask theater with the lively and stridently joyful energy of a street pageant. In their own words, HOBT's alchemy of "water, flour, newspaper, paint, and unlimited imagination" is harnessed to tell stories that explore the political and personal struggles and celebrations of human existence, from water issues to sustainable agriculture to grief and mourning.

Inspired by the social-justice stalwart Bread and Puppet Theater in Vermont, HOBT was started in 1973 in the basement of the Walker Church in Minneapolis' Powderhorn Park neighborhood. Today, the theater is still intimately linked to Powderhorn Park, which is the setting for its signature May Day Parade & Festival.

Held the first Sunday of May, the parade includes 2,000 people, many of them kids, who dance, bike, skate, sing, drum, strut, and twirl down Bloomington Avenue on their way to the Tree of Life Ceremony, which takes place in the park and culminates when the tens of thousands of attendees sing Gene Autry's "You Are My Sunshine." Part anarchist punk, part New Age flower child, the event is as much a commemoration of the workers of the world as it is an ode to spring. Add to that a crowd-induced exuberance that pumps out so many happy endorphins, and you'll think you are at a G-rated – okay, maybe PG-rated – carnival.

HOTB's work doesn't end there. In addition to live performances at their theater on Lake Street, they have a robust roster of touring productions, which can be performed in schools, day-care centers, libraries, and even birthday parties.

Address 1500 East Lake Street, Minneapolis, MN 55407, +1 (612)721-2535, www.hobt.org | Getting there Bus 21, 53 to Lake Street East and Bloomington Avenue South | Hours Mon–Fri 10am–4pm for office hours, show times vary | Tip Enjoy a different style of cutting-edge puppetry at Open Eye Figure Theater (506 East 24th Street, Minneapolis, MN 55404, www.openeyetheatre.org) in a beautifully restored 110-year-old venue.

48 Isles Studio

Homewares and haute taxidermy

A biology major, who went on to a career in the home design and garden industry, Jeff Bengtson has always had a passion for natural history. Isles Studio, his new shop in East Isles, is an extremely satisfying mind-meld of these two parts of Bengtson's brain. Part *Elle Decor*, part cabinet of curiosities, this is most definitely the only place in town where you can go home with a wool throw, a set of dessert plates, a skull, *and* a stuffed sacred ibis.

That's right: Bengtson specializes is extremely high-end taxidermy, including birds, insects, and even the stray reptile. And if taxidermy sets off your ethics alarm bells, rest easy. All the birds come either from zoos or sanctuaries and died of natural causes. An almost five-foot-tall sarus crane with head markings the color of a ripe apple lived until he was 40 at a California breeding program. Now he lords his beauty over a tablescape of coral – ethically harvested from a reef that had already died – a John Derian platter, a plaster foot, and a Grecian-style bust. Elsewhere, a parrot perches over a pile of coffee-table books and an emperor penguin protects a collection of scented candles.

Across the room, framed moths, chameleons, snakes, beetles, and butterflies by Oregon artist Christopher Marley challenge the viewer to see the beauty in things that make many of us squeamish. While Bengtson refreshes his homeware selection regularly – his collection of coffee-table books is especially strong – the taxidermy arrives on nature's schedule. At Isles Studio, you are never far from the circle of life. And given that each item is one of a kind, it is priced accordingly. That sarus crane, for example, will set you back $6,500. But there are plenty of treasures that fall into the impulse-buy category, and Bengtson is very welcoming toward browsers. "I put all my loves into one space," he says. "I want to bring inspiration to people who don't often get close to natural things."

Address 1311 West 25th Street, Minneapolis, MN 55405, +1 (612)999-4680, www.islesstudio.com | Getting there Bus 6, 12 to Hennepin Avenue and 25th Street West | Hours Call store for hours | Tip Extend your hunt for natural curiosities at Victory, a gorgeous antique shop that mixes geodes, shells, and coral into its edit of leather-bound books, gilt mirrors, and vintage jewelry (3505 West 44th Street, Minneapolis, www.shopvictory.com).

49 James J. Hill House

How the empire builder lived

When you build a 36,000-square-foot mansion, it's a safe bet that at least a part of your soul wants that house to say, "I'm rich!" The guests who, dwarfed by the size of your pile, will conclude, "And I'm not." That's certainly the verdict visitors reach when they step past the heavy oak doors of this Richardsonian Romanesque-style home that railway magnate James J. Hill commissioned for his family. He and his wife, Mary, lived there for 30 years, raising eight of their children in what was the largest home in the state when they moved there in 1891.

Set on Summit Avenue across the street from the St. Paul Cathedral, the James J. Hill House is now owned by the Minnesota Historical Society, which faithfully shows visitors how the Hills lived, down to the carbon filter light bulbs, which cast a glow that's dimmer than a birthday candle inside a pumpkin. It's odd to stand in spaces that are opulent even by today's standards yet shrouded in darkness because of the limits of technology in their day.

Still, you can't escape the markers of extreme wealth, including a pipe organ and elaborately carved paneling. In fact, the highest paid of the over 200 workers who built the home was Johannes Kirchmayer, a woodcarver from Bavaria who immortalized himself in a self-portrait hidden amidst the flourishes near the mansion's front door. Take a closer look, and you should be able to spot him.

As with most historic homes, it's the everyday details that draw you in, from the schoolroom on the third floor to the steel security gates that fold into slots in the wall. But perhaps the most interesting part of the Hill house is the basement, where you can visit the kitchen and the servants' dining room. When Hill died in 1916 he was the tenth richest man in America. But standing in his home, you realize the people you want to learn more about are the men and women who ironed his clothes and served his meals.

Address 240 Summit Avenue, St. Paul, MN 55102, +1 (651)297-2555, www.sites.mnhs.org/historic-sites/james-j-hill-house | **Getting there** Bus 21 to Selby and Summit Avenues or bus 63 to Smith Avenue and Walnut Street | **Hours** Guided tours Wed–Sat 10am–4pm, Sun 1–4pm | **Tip** In downtown St. Paul, check out Hill's gift to the city, the James J. Hill Center, a business library and reference center. While the center is currently closed, the exterior is glorious (80 West 4th Street, St. Paul, MN 55102, www.jjhill.org).

50__Karmel Mall

The first Somali mall in North America

In 2005, entrepreneur Basim Sabri opened the first Somali mall in North America to serve the needs of the quarter of the US Somali population who call the Twin Cities home. Given that the mall has grown from a handful of stalls in an old machine shop to almost 100,000 square feet, which includes 200 businesses and a 5,000-square-foot mosque, it was an inspired decision. Today, the two buildings that make up the south Minneapolis establishment next to the Midtown Greenway literally buzz with the chatter of people socializing, eating and doing business. That is, until the call to prayer blares through the speakers, and the place turns silent. And then, when the prayers are completed, it flips the switch and turns back on again.

There are food stalls that specialize in halal meats, including camel. And there are no-frills restaurants where you can order kebabs and *sambusas* and eat them underneath the glare of a flat-screen TV broadcasting an international soccer match. You can buy jewelry, cell phones, egg-stuffed potatoes, and *malawah*, a Somali pancake that's more like a crepe than something you'd slather in maple syrup and butter. And the clothes: rows and rows and rows of *abaya*s, *hijabs*, *diracs*, long skirts, and *baatis*.

Interestingly, all but a handful of the shops are owned and run by women. That includes Stall 110, which is Sabrina Seyf's henna parlour. Seyf's lacey designs are so sought after that customers fly her to their weddings and events. Even Venus Williams is a fan.

But despite her popularity, Seyf keeps her prices more reasonable than what you might pay at a suburban mall, which keeps her in very high demand. But, as she told Racked.com, that's because, for her, the 5,000-year-old tradition is as much about love as it is money. The same can also be said about Karmel Mall – it is in fact more than a mall, it's a living chronicle of a diaspora.

Address 2936–2944 Pillsbury Avenue South, Minneapolis, MN 55408, +1 (780)381-4293, www.karmelmall.com | **Getting there** Bus 21, 53, 18 to Lake Street West and Blaisdell Avenue South | **Hours** Unrestricted | **Tip** Visit The Somali Museum of Minnesota, the first Somali art museum in North America (1516 East Lake Street, Minneapolis, MN 55407, www.somalimuseum.org). They have a vibrant resident artists program.

51 Kayaking the Mississippi
Paddle in a national park

Maybe it's because we're focused on being the land of (over) 10,000 lakes, but most Twin Citians are shocked to discover the little-publicized fact that our stretch of the Mississippi River is actually a national park. Winding 72 miles from Ramsey in the north metro to Hastings near the Wisconsin border, the river's trails and parks offer a range of outdoor activities, from the wild northern shores, to the skyscraper views of Minneapolis, to the barges and tugboats that chug through St. Paul's working river.

While the network of hiking and biking trails are world class, the most unique way to get a fresh perspective on our river – and also the cities that owe their existences to it – is to get out on the water, preferably in a canoe or a kayak, where you can appreciate the scale of both the river and our urban landscape from the pin drop quiet of the water. If you have any experience with kayaking, the Mississippi Paddle Share program allows you to rent kayaks and life vests at self-service stations in North Mississippi Regional Park in Brooklyn Park and the Mississippi Watershed Management Organization near the Lowry Avenue Bridge. Then you can paddle downstream to Boom Island Regional Park in Northeast Minneapolis to return the equipment. It takes approximately 85 minutes to kayak from Brooklyn Park and 45 from the Lowry Avenue Bridge. If you aren't up for paddling back upstream, you can either call an Uber car or rent a bike from Boom Island's Nice Ride station.

If that sounds like too much of an expedition to take on your own, several outfitters offer excellent guided tours. Above the Falls (www.abovethefallssports.com) takes you on a four-hour adventure from Coon Rapids to downtown Minneapolis. Craving something a little more social? Wilderness Inquiry (www.wildernessinquiry.org) sends groups down the river in their 24-foot cedar-strip canoes, which hold 9 paddlers.

Address North Mississippi Regional Park, 5700 North Lyndale Avenue, Brooklyn Center, MN 55430, +1 (763)694-7790, www.threeriversparks.org/location/north-mississippi-regional-park); Mississippi Watershed Management Organization, 2522 Marshall Street Northeast, Minneapolis, MN 55418, +1 (612)746-4970, www.mwmo.org | **Getting there** North Mississippi River Regional Park: Bus 22 to the Bryant and 49th Avenues North and walk towards Lyndale Avenue North. Mississippi Watershed Management Organization: Bus 32 to Lowry Avenue and Marshall Street Northeast. | **Hours** See websites for guided tour and Paddle Share schedules | **Tip** Above the Falls (www.abovethefallssports.com) also runs Friday evening sunset paddles from North Mississippi Regional Park to Boom Island. Times vary according to sunset.

52 Kenilworth Channel

A Monet landscape in Minneapolis

A canal that links the grandeur of Lake of the Isles' mansions with the wooded seclusion of Cedar Lake, Kenilworth Channel is a secret idyll that's so picturesque you'll think you've stepped into one of Monet's water lily masterpieces. If you're lucky, you might even spot a great blue heron swooping, pterodactyl-style, over the cattails.

Best experienced from the water, the channel is a favorite of canoeists, kayakers, and paddle boarders, who literally can't stop themselves from grinning as they marvel at a quiet that's disturbed only by the splash of an oar slicing the water or the caws of birds nesting in the trees that arch overhead. It's one of the most remote spots in town and gives you a fresh perspective on why it's special to live in the city of lakes.

Head west under the Beaux Arts-style bridge at Lake of the Isles – watch out for the teenagers who've been (illegally) jumping into the canal for decades, if not generations – and make your way to Cedar Lake and its Hidden Beach, which has long been a favorite of the clothing-optional crew. If that's not your scene, don't worry: stay in the middle of the lake and take a swim. (The water in the canal itself is a bit too mucky to feel refreshing.) If your arms aren't zonked, keep paddling west, where you'll spot a hole in a wall that's actually a bridge to Brownie Lake, the most remote and rustic pond in the city.

When you turn back, float east through the canal and pass under an old timber bridge – set to be replaced by a much less charming concrete version if a new light-rail line gets the green light. Not only will you enjoy a glimpse at some of the city's loveliest backyards, you'll also see the skyscrapers of downtown shooting above the trees lining Lake of the Isles Boulevard. It's a vista that reminds every Minneapolitan that our city is a place where nature meets culture with stunning success.

Address The channel starts at the corner of West Lake of the Isles Boulevard and Dean Parkway. | **Getting there** Bus 12, 17 to Lake Street West and Bde Maka Ska Parkway to rent a paddleboard. | **Hours** Kenilworth Channel is open 24 hours a day. Wheel Fun Rental hours are Mon–Fri 9am–7:30pm, Sat–Sun 8am–7:30pm. Open from May 28–Labor Day. | **Tip** Most people rent a canoe, paddle board, or kayak at Wheel Fun Rentals, located at the northwestern edge of Bde Maka Ska (3000 Bde Maka Ska Parkway, Minneapolis, MN 55408, www.wheelfunrentals.com/Locations/Minneapolis).

53 Kramarczuk's

Sausages, sausages, and more sausages

Let us stop for a moment to consider the sausage. A humble combination of leftover pig parts and intestines, it's perhaps the yummiest example ever of food upcycling, which is perhaps why so many countries have their own much-adored version. An overwhelming selection of this celebrated foodstuff can be found at Kramarczuk's, the Eastern European specialty store on East Hennepin in Minneapolis. Münchner weisswurst, English bangers, linguiça, kielbasa, wild rice brats, tea sausage, andouille – the list goes on. And on.

Founded in 1954 by Wasyl and Anna Kramarczuk, who immigrated to the US in the late 1940s from the Ukraine, Kramarczuk's has been holding down the fort on the other side of the Hennepin Avenue bridge from downtown since long before the neighborhood became popular with the lawyers and professors who now live in the area's lofts and condos. Wasyl made the sausages. Anna was in charge of the baked goods.

We certainly must thank the heavens for Anna! Her *kolachi* is a gorge-worthy pillow of dough stuffed with fruit preserves, and her chocolate babka and *potica* (a rolled dough cake filled with sweet nuts) are epic. These treats are not common; you often have to go to smaller towns with Eastern European roots to find them.

Kramarczuk's also has a restaurant, where you can feast on *pierogi* (like everything else, they're handmade on site), cabbage rolls, Ukrainian meatballs, and *bigos*, which is a sweet-and-sour hunter's stew made with pork, sausage, sauerkraut, and onions, all of which have such a loyal following that the Kramarczuk family has published their own cookbook. The restaurant also offers the deli standards, from a Reuben sandwich to a pastrami brisket, and a satisfying selection of Polish and Czech beers. If you are a hunter, the Kramarczuk's butchers will mix your wild game with pork for your own custom beer sticks and summer sausages. *Poyisty!*

Address 215 East Hennepin Avenue, Minneapolis, MN 55414, +1 (612)379-3081, www.kramarczuks.com | Getting there Bus 4, 6, to East Hennepin Avenue and 2nd Street Northeast | Hours Mon–Wed 8am–8pm, Thu–Sat 8am–9pm, Sun 10am–4pm | Tip Minneapolis is the home of Aveda, the national holistic skin and body products company, which was founded by Minnesota-transplant and natural beauty visionary Horst Rechel-bacher. Visit the original Aveda Arts & Sciences Institute (400 Central Avenue South-east, Minneapolis, MN 55414, www.avedaarts.edu/guest/services), a training center for aestheticians, for a mani/pedi or any number of pampering services performed by students and their supervisors, at significantly discounted prices.

54 Lakewood Cemetery

Tiptoe through the tombstones

Imagine being shrunk, "I Dream of Jeannie"-style, so that you're the size of one tiny ruby inside Queen Elizabeth's jewelry box. That's the feeling you'll get when you enter the Lakewood Memorial Chapel in Lakewood Cemetery on the southeastern shore of Bde Maka Ska in Minneapolis. Completed in 1910 and designed by local architect Harry Wild Jones (who also was the brains behind the Washburn Park water tower and Minneapolis' Butler Square), this National Historic Register stunner was inspired by the Hagia Sophia in Istanbul.

Inside, the chapel is covered in a Byzantine mosaic design in a technique you'll also find in Venice's San Marco Cathedral. It's considered one of the best of its kind in the United States. The 6th-century-meets-art-nouveau tableaux were created by New York interior designer Charles Lamb, who traveled to Rome to hire six of Italy's most respected mosaic artists to create more than 10 million mosaic pieces from marble, colored stone, and glass flecked with gold and silver. If no one is around, stand near the altar and start talking. The acoustics are so perfect you won't need a mike to be heard.

The only slight buzzkill in all this gorgeousness is that the chapel is used primarily for funerals. That's because it's smack in the middle of the Minneapolis graveyard, which is the final resting place of, among other notables: former US Senator and Vice President Hubert H. Humphrey; US Senator Paul Wellstone and his wife, Sheila, who died in a tragic plane accident in the last stretch of his senatorial campaign; Franklin C. Mars, the inventor of the Mars Bar; and Herbert Buckingham Khaury, better known as Tiny Tim, who was famous for singing "Tiptoe Through The Tulips" in a falsetto while playing the ukulele. The cemetery also has a special section called Showman's Rest, for circus performers who've gone to the Big Top in the sky.

Address 3600 Hennepin Avenue, Minneapolis, MN 55408, +1 (612)822-2171, www.lakewoodcemetery.com | Getting there Bus 6 or 23 to Hennepin Avenue South and 36th Street West | Hours Chapel: Mon – Sat 8am – 4:30pm, if locked, ask someone at the administration building to let you in; cemetery grounds: see website | Tip Six blocks down on 36th Street near Bryant Avenue South, taste test the artsy offerings (lavender cake, dark chocolate ganache) at Bogart's Doughnut Co. (904 West 36th Street, Minneapolis, MN 55408, www.bogartsdoughnutco.com).

55_ The Landing

Olde tyme traditions on the Minnesota

"Did you arrive by stage?" is a question you probably don't get asked very often, especially by a teacher who is dressed up like she's Laura Ingalls Wilder. Odds are you arrived by car, but the question will begin your immersion into the experience of visiting The Landing – Minnesota River Heritage Park, an 88-acre open-air museum that depicts life in the Lower Minnesota River Valley from the 1840s to 1890s.

Located 24 miles from downtown Minneapolis on a bend in the Minnesota River east of Shakopee, The Landing (formerly Murphy's Landing) includes authentic 19th-century buildings, including Major Murphy's Inn, a grist mill, a blacksmith shop, a one-room schoolhouse, a chapel, and farmsteads. All are open to visitors and you can talk with "farmers" about their heritage crops and the recipes they're cooking on wood-burning stoves. You can also try your hand at writing old German script – the language of the region back in the day – on the schoolhouse slate blackboard. The interpreters, who rarely break character, are experts on the traditions of the region as well as the history of the buildings.

Now run by the Three Rivers Park District, The Landing's hours vary depending on the season, and the attractions change accordingly. Spring is all about maple sugar and syrup making, whereas December is a full-on holiday fest, with traditions from the area's settlers, which include Czech, Slovak, Finnish, French Canadian, German Moravian, German, Irish, Jewish, Norwegian, and Swedish. If you are a fan of Victorian Christmas carols (and men with mutton chops singing them), this is your scene.

Best of all, The Landing is the perfect place to take in views of the Minnesota River, a gentle waterway and the state's namesake that gets much less attention than the big river it runs into. There's even an overlook wall that was constructed by the Works Progress Administration.

Address 2187 Highway 101 East, Shakopee, MN 55379, +1 (763)694-7784, www.threeriversparks.org/parks/the-landing.aspx | Getting there From Minneapolis and St. Paul, take US 169 South to the exit for MN-13/Savage/Hennepin County/Shakopee | Hours See website, vary by season | Tip During the fall, head 2 miles east on Highway 101 to the corn maze at Sever's Fall Festival. There's also a pumpkin patch for your Halloween jack-o-lanterns (1100 Canterbury Road South, Shakopee, MN 55379, seversfallfestival.com).

56 Little Mekong
Southeast Asia in St. Paul

Named for the river that flows from China through Myanmar, Laos, Cambodia, and Vietnam, this busy section of St. Paul's Frogtown neighborhood has become a prime business and cultural district for the Southeast Asian community. Stretching from MacKubin and Galtier Streets on University Avenue, the area is home to restaurants, bakeries, grocers, and service businesses.

Little Mekong got its start in the 1970s, when Hmong, Cambodian, Vietnamese, Lao, and Thai civilians fled their countries in the wake of the Vietnam War. Minnesota welcomed them to the point where today the state has the second largest Hmong population in the country. Some of those settlers set up shop on University Avenue.

Today, the easiest and decidedly most enjoyable way to experience this district is through its food. Start with a bowl of traditional Vietnamese beef noodles at Pho Ca Dao (439 University Avenue West). Served with a side plate of fresher-than-fresh Thai basil, bean sprouts, jalapenos, lime and *culantro* (a robust herb that's similar in taste to cilantro), it's the ultimate comfort food, where the layers of textures and flavors are released into the broth. The restaurant itself is the opposite of fancy (it's a hole-in-the-wall, actually), and they don't accept checks or credit cards, so adjust your expectations and habits accordingly.

Pho Ca Dao also serves rainbow-like three-color desserts (a kind of parfait of agar jelly, beans, and coconut milk). For some truly elegant choices, head east on University to Marc Heu Patisserie Paris (383 University Avenue West, www.marcheuparis.com) to sample anything from a slice of Paris brest to a chocolate-pistachio-cream pastry.

The district is also known for its annual summer Night Market. Like its Southeast Asian counterparts, it's a relaxed open-air bazaar where you can get bubble tea and artisan crafts, and watch live performances.

Address University Avenue, St. Paul, MN 55103 (between MacKubin and Galtier Streets) | **Getting there** Metro to Western Avenue (Green Line) or bus 16 to University Avenue and Arundel Street | **Hours** Unrestricted | **Tip** For a more upscale dining experience, Ngon Vietnamese Bistro offers a delicious blend of Vietnamese and French cuisines (799 University Avenue West, St. Paul, MN 55104, www.ngonbistro.com).

57 Luminary Loppet

Walking (and skiing) in a winter wonderland

If there's a single event that captures Minnesotans' budding determination to see our intense and sometimes unforgiving winters as a cultural asset, it's the Luminary Loppet, which is held each winter, either in late January or early February, on Lake of the Isles in Minneapolis. A nighttime cross-country ski trek where the path is lit only by ice lanterns, the celebration is a joyous, if not chilly, revel, complete with live music, fire jugglers, hot cocoa and s'more stations, and handmade ice pyramids. There's even an "IceHenge" circle of frosty, candlelit slabs, where you can stop to make a wish, think deep thoughts, or plot your way to the beer tent. Whatever you do, dress for the cold because you won't want to head back indoors. Of course, that is the whole point of this event.

Founded in 2006 as an all-ages street-party-on-ice to support the other more physically challenging Loppet sporting events that take place that weekend, the Luminary's outsize success – participants now ski the course in several different waves throughout the evening and others walk or show shoe – has spawned its own subcultures beyond the Nordic ski types flying by in their Lycra bodysuits. Those fire jugglers, with their leather vests and tatts, are straight out of "Mad Max" and the fixie bike scene. On the more patrician end of the spectrum, some families who live on or near Lake of the Isles host special Loppet parties, where friends grab a bite to eat and warm up in front of the fireplace before continuing on the trail or heading to another party to catch up with a different set of pals.

It's a scene so whimsical you'll feel like you've landed in a fairy tale, without the threat of an evil witch trying to stuff you into an oven – truly a stunning reminder of the magic that can happen in cold and dark places. Kids love it, but there's so much for the child-free that you won't feel like you're stuck at Sesame Street Live. This is *the* happening of the year that you don't want to miss.

Address Lake of the Isles, Minneapolis, www.loppet.org/luminary-loppet | Getting there
Park around or near Lake of the Isles. You can also park in Uptown and walk to Lake of
the Isles or take a shuttle bus from the Walker Library, which is served by the 6, 12 to
Hennepin Avenue and Uptown Station. | **Hours** The event starts at 6pm. | **Tip** Start your
night by skating outdoors on the Lake of the Isles rink, a slice of Norman Rockwell's
America, complete with bumpy ice and the shockingly loud *thwap* of hockey pucks
slapping against the boards (2500 Lake of the Isles Parkway East, Minneapolis, MN 55405,
www.minneapolisparks.org).

58 Maiden Lane

Look into the backyards of the Gilded Age

Running through the middle of residential blocks that stretch from Western Avenue to the Cathedral of St. Paul in that city's Cathedral Hill neighborhood, Maiden Lane feels more like an alley than an actual street. Unlike the surrounding roads, it's still paved in cobblestones. While it's not a well-known attraction compared to all the Cass Gilbert mansions and other historic homes nearby, this hidden street gives you more of a feel for what an ordinary person's life was like in the 1890s because it still rests where many of the mansions' carriage and coach houses were located.

Several of the carriage houses are meticulously restored as single-family homes and apartments. The stunning, red brick 260 Maiden Lane was built in 1891 and served as the carriage house for the James J. Hill house, which is over a block away on Summit Avenue. Apparently, Hill realized too late that his massive lot overlooking the Mississippi River was on too steep of a slope to accommodate the carriage house, which is why it's not more conveniently located. Like the Hill House, the carriage house is also gigantic at almost 4,000 square feet. It was built with bricks from a previous Hill house and is now a private residence. But the most charming home is 297 Maiden Lane, which was the former boiler house for a Laurel Terrace rowhouse. At just 1,040 square feet, it feels like a gray brick dollhouse. At night, the lamplight from all the homes along the lane casts an especially magical glow.

As you walk toward the Cathedral, on your right you'll pass by the backyard of the Germanic-American Institute. This cultural center, located in a 1906 mansion, which was a priory in the 1950s and 1960s, boast a *ratskeller* and offers German classes and a range of other events and activities, such as waltz lessons and film screenings. The Institute also hosts an annual Oktoberfest celebration, which is open to the public (www.gai-mn.org).

Address One block off Summit Avenue, between Western Avenue and the Cathedral of St. Paul, St. Paul, MN 55102 | **Getting there** Bus 21 to Selby and Summit Avenues | **Hours** Unrestricted | **Tip** Visit the Cathedral of St. Paul and towards the back, look for the Shrine of Nations, made up of tiny chapels honoring the six European ethnic groups that settled the city (239 Selby Avenue, St. Paul, MN 55102, www.cathedralsaintpaul.org).

59 __ Manhole Covers

Art underfoot

With all of central downtown Minneapolis' woes, with the closing of flagship stores like Macy's and Barnes and Noble, and the construction on Nicollet Mall, it's tempting to dismiss this once beloved urban center as nothing more than a place where people work and then flee. But in addition to being overly dramatic – the North Loop and the Mill District, after all, are booming – those complaints ignore the fact that the city contains forgotten delights that, while they won't generate economic activity, will still delight.

Case in point: the artist-designed manhole covers that are scattered up and down Nicollet and across 6th Street and 7th Street between Nicollet and Hennepin. The first batch was commissioned in the 1980s to explore the theme of entertainment in the city. On 6th Street, David Atkinson's homage to Minnesota summers comes in the form of a grill loaded with brats, burgers, and onions. On 7th Street, photographer Stuart Klipper's commentary on the concept of "X marks the spot" tells viewers to "KNOW WHERE YOU ARE" and "BE WHERE YOU'RE AT," an idea that's worth pondering as you get on and off the bus on your daily commute. And while there are a few head-scratchers – the dancing girls kicking like Rockettes seems more suited to a manhole cover in front of Radio City Music Hall – it's a kick to see "Minneapolis City of Lakes" spelled out in cursive over splashes that are actually shaped like our urban lakes.

The city commissioned 11 more manhole designs by Pennsylvania artist Kate Burke to replace 75 covers on Nicollet Mall, which were installed in 1992. Made from cast iron, *Hail Minnesota* is a series of elaborate relief carvings depicting state icons; a loon, lady slippers, and overlapping boughs of a Norway pine. If you think they sound cliché, you're not wrong, but keep looking. Burke included subtle surprises to keep viewers on their toes.

Address Nicollet Mall and 6th and 7th Street in downtown Minneapolis | Getting there Bus 14, 94 to 6th Street and Nicollet Mall | Hours Unrestricted | Tip One of the most iconic scenes in television history was filmed on the corner of 7th Street and Nicollet Mall in Minneapolis, where beloved actress Mary Tyler Moore tossed her blue-striped tam high into the air for the opening credits of her eponymous TV show. She certainly made it all seem worthwhile.

60 Marshall Terrace Rookery

Where birds of a feather flock together

When a deadly tornado churned through north Minneapolis in the spring of 2011, the devastation didn't just impact the people whose houses and businesses were demolished. Approximately 200 great blue herons also lost their nests when their rookery on an island in North Mississippi Regional Park was badly damaged, and the cottonwood trees the birds called home were blown down. Birdwatchers didn't know when or how the herons could rebuild their home.

The adult herons saw the storm coming and many were able to get out of harm's way. A rescue operation saved one adult blue heron and 13 chicks, which were released back into the wild. But the birds abandoned their rookery. Then, a month later, the staff at Xcel Energy noticed that dozens of blue herons had established a new home on islands in the Mississippi across from the Riverside Plant, next to Marshall Terrace Park in Northeast Minneapolis.

They are still there, and if the sight doesn't inspire you to contemplate the resilience and beauty of these magnificent creatures, then your soul might need a reboot. To see them for yourself, head over to Marshall Terrace Park in Northeast and walk past the baseball diamond and towards the river. There's a paved trail that leads to a wooden staircase, which takes you down to the water. It's a stretch of the Mississippi that's more industrial than the historically preserved warehouses of downtown, but look toward the islands and you'll soon make out dark puffs perched high in the branches, like lollipops in the sky. Those are the nests.

Keep watching! Before long the puffs will move, and you'll see the herons stand and stretch their necks. Stay longer, and one will decide it's time for some fishing and flap, flap, flap its way down the river, its claws pointed with the precision of a ballerina. The best time to spot them is March and April, when they return for the warm months, and there are no leaves on the trees.

Address Marshall Terrace Park, 2740 Marshall Street Northeast, Minneapolis, MN 55418, +1 (612)568-7422, www.marshallterrace.org/heron-cam.html | Getting there Bus 11 to Grand Street and 27th Avenue Northeast or bus 32 to Lowry Avenue and Marshall Street Northeast | Hours Daily 6am–midnight | Tip Visit The Raptor Center, where more than 700 injured or sick eagles, falcons, and hawks are rehabilitated every year (1920 Fitch Avenue, St. Paul, MN 55108, www.raptor.umn.edu). The "Raptors of Minnesota" program runs every weekend at 1pm.

61 Marion and University

Where Homer Van Meter got popped

On July 22, 1934, gangster John Dillinger was gunned down by FBI agents in front of the Biograph Theater in Chicago. When Homer Van Meter, Dillinger's partner in crime, heard the news on the radio, he fled with his girlfriend Marie Conforti to Minnesota.

Their first hideout was the Leech Lake Log Cabin Camp near Walker, according to Paul Maccabee's *John Dillinger Slept Here: A Crook's Tour of Crime and Corruption in St. Paul.* But Van Meter would sneak into St. Paul for "meets" with his associates at bars and bowling alleys on Rice Street. They moved around to other resorts, where Van Meter, who'd had plastic surgery to disguise his identity before Dillinger was killed, fished and Conforti swam.

Then, on August 23, Van Meter was back in St. Paul. Disguised with a moustache, a blue serge suit, and a straw hat, he walked out of St. Paul Motors to a car that was parked on Marion Street just north of University Avenue. That's when the police, armed with two sawed-off shotguns and two machine guns, shouted, "Stick 'em up!"

Van Meter fired a .38 Colt automatic over his shoulder and took off, running south on University toward an alley near Aurora Avenue. Unfortunately for him, it was a blind alley. That's when, according to Maccabee, a blast of buckshot from one of the shotguns sent Van Meter two feet into the air. He died slumped against a garage wall between Aurora and Marion, with 50 bullets in his body and $923 in his pocket.

Today, the site of this grisly event is a treeless corner, bordered by a McDonald's, a Sunrise Banks outpost, King Thai Restaurant, and an empty lot. But you still get an idea of what Van Meter saw in his final moments. Look south on Marion, and you'll spot the Cathedral of St. Paul. To the east, you can see the Minnesota State Capitol. Both were just a few decades old on that day, and you can only imagine the stories they could tell.

Address University Avenue and Marion Street, St. Paul, MN 55103 | Getting there
Bus 16 to University Avenue and Marion Street or LRT Green Line to Capitol/Rice
Street | Hours Unrestricted | Tip In downtown St. Paul, the castle-like Landmark Center
(75th 5th Street West, St. Paul, MN 55102, www.landmarkcenter.org), which used to be a
courthouse, was where John Dillinger's girlfriend, Evelyn Frechette, and also Doc Barker,
the gangster son of the notorious Ma Barker, were both tried. A former bellboy who got
involved with gangsters is said to haunt the Landmark Center, where he has been seen
most often on the third floor.

62 The Mary Tyler Moore House

TV's most famous bachelorette pad

Who can turn the world on with her smile? If you are a fan of classic sitcoms, you'll know that the answer is Mary Richards, the plucky protagonist of the groundbreaking "The Mary Tyler Moore Show," which aired from 1970 to 1977. She could definitely take a nothing day and suddenly make it all seem worthwhile.

While the series was filmed at CBS Studio Center in Los Angeles, it was fictitiously set in Minneapolis, and the opening title sequences were shot at local landmarks. Locals of a certain age may remember what a big deal it was when Moore came to town and pretended to shop in the meat section of the now defunct Red Owl grocery store (which was also referenced in the Coen Brothers film *A Serious Man*), passed by a school crossing guard, and tossed her hat in the air on Nicollet Mall in a rush of career woman you're-going-to-make-it-after-all optimism.

The most famous of the show's locations is the massive Queen Anne Victorian mansion on Kenwood Parkway that was used as the exterior of the apartment building where Mary and her pal Rhoda rented out their bachelorette pads from landlady Phyllis Lindstrom. During the show's heyday, tour busses regularly pulled up so that fans could photograph the home. Some, not realizing the interior wasn't used for the show, knocked on the door for tours. This became such an inconvenience for the owner that she eventually put an "Impeach Nixon" sign on her lawn to discourage gawkers.

Today, as long as you are mindful that it's a private residence, you can walk past and even photograph the house. To make an outing of it, walk down Kenwood Parkway to the Peavey Fountain, a memorial to horses killed in action during World War I. Then do like Mary did and stride confidently around Lake of the Isles.

Address 2104 Kenwood Parkway, Minneapolis, MN 55405 | Getting there Bus 25 to 21st Street West and Kenwood Parkway | Hours Always accessible to view from outside | Tip A few blocks away on West 21st Street, stop in at Birchbark Books (2115 West 21st Street, Minneapolis, MN 55405, www.birchbarkbooks.com), an independent book and native crafts store that's owned by acclaimed author Louise Erdrich.

63 __ The Meat Raffle

The jackpot is bacon and porterhouse steaks

"TWELVE!" The wheel stops spinning, and the lucky number is shouted across the main room at Half Time Rec, the storied St. Paul dive bar that was featured in the movie *Grumpy Old Men*. The crowd, which is surprisingly robust considering it's 5:15pm on a Friday summer evening, looks down at their tiny white squares. Within seconds, a guy who is dressed like he just went through a bucket of golf balls at the municipal driving range throws his arms up. Woohoo! He's going home with a pair of porterhouse steaks.

The mistress of ceremonies threads through the crowd, carrying a tray of $1 tickets she's selling for the second round. There are still plenty of takers, all of whom are eager to bring home either the bacon, the beef kabobs, or the sausages that are waiting in a cardboard box in the other room. (The ground beef is usually the last to go.) When she steps up to the wheel again, people yell out their numbers with almost as much anticipation as if they were at a Vegas roulette table.

Welcome to the Meat Raffle, a gathering where butchers donate popular cuts of beef to local bars, who in turn host booze-fueled lotteries and donate the proceeds to charity – think bingo for carnivores. A Minnesota institution that used to be found mostly in rural areas, meat raffles have now taken hold in bars across the metro. Some say that's thanks to the recession, although when has the promise of an almost-free steak dinner *not* been appealing? A meat raffle makes happy hour even happier.

Known for its rowdy crowds and basement bocce courts, Half Time Rec is an institution in the neighborhood bar scene, especially when St. Patrick's Day rolls around every year. . But the weekly meat raffle is a tamer gathering, where you'll see a guy in a kilt sharing a laugh with a woman with overly bleached hair pulled into a ponytail and a server with Wednesday Addams tattooed on her calf. Meat, it seems, is a great unifier.

Address 1013 Front Avenue, St. Paul, MN 55103, +1 (651)488-8245, www.halftimerec.com | Getting there Bus 3 to Front Avenue and Oxford Street or Chatsworth Street | Hours Weekly Fri 5pm; bar: Mon–Fri 11am–2am, Sat & Sun 10am–2am | Tip If you get shut out at the raffle, head over to the St. Paul Meat Shop, the city's only whole-animal butcher to pick up your favorite cuts (1674 Grand Avenue, St. Paul, MN 55015, www.stpaulmeatshop.com).

64 Midtown Global Market

One stop shop for tacos, tarts, and tagines

In a state that's proud of its retail shops – we're talking about you, Target and Best Buy HQs – most people don't realize that after a modest start at a rail station in Redwood Falls, MN, Sears, Roebuck & Co used to have a prominent local presence too, thanks to the art moderne-style behemoth on Lake Street that housed the company's mail order warehouse and flagship Minneapolis store.

Sears moved out of that location in 1994, which unfortunately resulted in rough times for the area around Lake Street and Chicago Avenue. But, starting in 2006, the building and neighborhood got a second chance as the headquarters of Allina Hospitals and Clinics and the home of the Midtown Global Market.

An international-themed bazaar, Midtown Global Market is the only place in town where you can satisfy your craving for anything from tamales and *boba* smoothies, to *roti*, tagines, and coconut macaroons. Among the many standouts is Manny's Tortas, which specializes in gourmet Mexican sandwiches. And don't miss Hot Indian Foods, which specializes in the "Indurrito," an Indian burrito.

It's a happy scene that's great for a first date. And parents can relax when their kids jump up to dance to the live music or run to get a second bottle of brightly colored Jarritos Mexican soda. In a city where winter can last as long as five months, Midtown Global Market is an indoor public square that specializes in the non-generic, non-chain store shopping opportunities that you won't find at a mall.

Originally envisioned as an incubator for neighborhood-bred ethnic businesses, Midtown Global Market has had its share of successes and disappointments. But after a decade of hard work, the food vendors, entertainers, grocers, and gift-shop owners have accomplished something even bigger than building profitable shops and restaurants. They've helped revive a neighborhood.

Address 920 East Lake Street, Minneapolis, MN 55407, +1 (612)872-4041, www.midtownglobalmarket.org | Getting there Bus 21 to Lake Street East and 10th Avenue South or bus 5 to Chicago Lake Transit Center and Gate A | Hours Mon – Sat 7am – 8pm, Sun 10am – 6pm | Tip Take in a play or visit a community art project at Pillsbury House Theatre (3501 Chicago Avenue South, Minneapolis, MN 55407, www.pillsburyhouseandtheatre.org).

65 Midtown Greenway
The power of the pedal

With over 200 miles of on- and off-street bikeways, Minneapolis has certainly earned its bragging rights as one of the country's top cities for cycling, even when the paths are glossed with ice or clotted with snow. This 5.66-mile section of the Grand Rounds Scenic Byway System is a particularly fine example of what makes urban biking such a satisfying way to commute (no stop lights!), not to mention exercise away from the fluorescent glare of the gym.

Situated in a former railroad corridor that had deteriorated into a trench clogged with trash, the Midtown Greenway came to life in 2000, when a portion of the rail bed just east of St. Louis Park was paved to connect to Lake of the Isles, Bde Maka Ska, and Hennepin. Today, the trail stretches from the Chain of Lakes all the way to the Mississippi River, passing through an economically and ethnically diverse range of neighborhoods, from Kenwood, to Lyn-Lake, to Whittier, to Longfellow.

While there's plenty of leafy allure, the real magic of riding the length of the Greenway is how every block reveals the dynamic beauty of our city landscape. Because it's literally in what was once the guts of the city – much of the corridor is below street level – you experience the neighborhoods from the inside instead of their more public façades. You glide under timeworn bridges, pass the backsides of warehouses and distribution centers, and then work up a sweat as you ascend over the blare of Hiawatha via the Martin Olav Sabo Bridge, which happens to be the first cable-stayed suspension bridge in the state.

Along the way you'll see community gardens, a soccer pitch, community-sponsored murals, and other surprises, including a bench with a pair of abandoned shoes that upon closer inspection are actually a permanent piece of art. No matter how many times you set out on this trail, there will be something new to discover.

Address The Trail runs parallel to Lake Street, with over 2-dozen access points, www.midtowngreenway.com | Getting there Visit the website for a map, access points, and distances | Hours Unrestricted | Tip Keep pedaling to other points of interest along the Grand Rounds Scenic Byway System (www.minneapolisparks.org).

66 Mill City Museum

An explosively good time

Built into the ruins of what was once the world's largest flour mill, this museum – which is devoted to the surprisingly compelling ways the flour industry and the Mississippi River combined to create an economy that built modern-day Minneapolis – has a dramatic backstory. Back in 1878, when the building was known as the Washburn A Mill (Washburn-Crosby brands would go on to become General Mills), a spark ignited airborne flour dust, which created an explosion that was so powerful it leveled the building and started a fire that destroyed much of the riverfront business area and cut the city's milling capacity in half. Even more tragic, 18 people died in the accident.

A safer and more productive mill was rebuilt – at its peak, it was milling enough flour to produce 12 million loaves of bread a day – but that building was also damaged by a fire in 1990, after being closed for 25 years. That's when the Minnesota Historical Society stepped in and repurposed the brick-and-beam warehouse into a museum. The decision was an ingenious and important one for the city, because a visit to the Mill City Museum is a fascinating look at how industry and nature helped to create our thriving slice of the Midwest.

While the entire museum, from the baking lab (with free samples) to the film *Minneapolis in 19 Minutes Flat*, which is narrated by humorist Kevin Kling, is more than worth your time, don't miss the Flour Tower. An eight-minute freight elevator ride where you experience different aspects of the mill's history on each floor, it culminates with a dramatic – and loud – surprise. When your cortisol rush settles, you can visit the 9th-floor observation deck, which offers lovely views of the river, St. Anthony Falls, Stone Arch Bridge, and the rapidly expanding city. At night, the mill's Gold Medal Flour signage shines bright, a reminder to all of how our city got its start.

Address 704 South 2nd Street, Minneapolis, MN 55401, +1 (612)341-7555, www.millcitymuseum.org | Getting there Bus 7, 22 to Washington Avenue South and Park Avenue | Hours Tue – Sat 10am – 5pm, Sun noon – 5pm | Tip The historic Mill Ruins Park (102 Portland Avenue South, Minneapolis, MN 55401) is equal parts natural beauty and archeological treasures that tell the story of the mills in Minneapolis.

67 Milwaukee Avenue

An homage to the common man's architecture

Why would you make a point of visiting a little-known patch of inward-facing blocks just off Franklin Avenue in Minneapolis' Seward neighborhood? Because a walk down this two-block stretch of modest brick homes on what was originally called 22 ½ Avenue is a stroll back in time where you get a peek not at the homes of the titans of Twin Cities industry, but the workers who helped them succeed.

Milwaukee Avenue was built between 1884 and 1890 by real estate speculator William Ragan, who maximized his investment by building on quarter lots and using identical house plans and materials. Intended for workers and their families, the brick-and-clapboard homes are accented with gabled roofs, arched windows, and front porches laced with gingerbread trim. The houses' first residents were mostly immigrants from Northern Europe, many of whom worked in the nearby rail yards and industrial shops.

The Depression and two World Wars took their toll on the neighborhood, which declined to the point where the city planned to raze it in 1970. That's when residents of Milwaukee Avenue and the Seward neighborhood, many of whom had honed their protesting chops during the Vietnam War, banded together to save the street. When the city didn't appreciate their argument that the homes were historically significant, the neighborhood committee secretly applied to the National Register of Historic Places, which approved the request in 1974.

Today, the homes on Milwaukee Avenue have been faithfully restored to reflect their 19th-century beginnings and "common man's" architectural style. Taken together, they look like a model train neighborhood or a town from a movie set. At a time where the community – enhancing concepts of New Urbanism are touted as a way to save our sprawling McMansion-filled suburbs, Milwaukee Avenue's front porches prove that the old ways can be the best ways.

Address Franklin Avenue East between 22nd and 23rd Avenues, Minneapolis, MN 55404 | Getting there Metro to Franklin Avenue (Blue Line) or bus 2 to Franklin Avenue East and 22nd Avenue South | Hours Unrestricted from the outside only | Tip Head west on Franklin and check out the Seward Community Coop, a community anchor since it opened in 1972 (2823 East Franklin Avenue, Minneapolis, MN 55406, www.seward.coop).

68 Minneapolis American Indian Center

Urban heart of the Native community

One of the first urban organizations of its kind in the country, Minneapolis American Indian Center (MAIC) has been providing services to the city's American Indian community since 1974. Part of the American Indian Cultural Corridor on Franklin Avenue in Minneapolis, MAIC is both a gathering place and art space, where you can take in a gallery show or enjoy a delicious meal.

Gatherings Café serves healthy, indigenous food: a bison melt seasoned with a tangy blueberry sauce, or a hand-harvested bowl of wild rice topped with kale, mushrooms and homemade candied seeds. The menu is both tasty and an intentional counterbalance to a colonial food industry that has led to high rates of obesity, diabetes, and heart disease in the Native population. Gatherings is part of the local Native-foods movement, which includes Tatanka Trunk (tatankatruck.com), an award-winning food truck serving food from Native food producers in Minnesota and the Dakotas.

Woodland Indian Crafts specializes in handmade beaded jewelry. Owner Charlie Stately learned how to bead when he was a child at a South Dakota boarding school. "I was good at school, but creating traditional art was always the thing that interested me the most," he says. Today, Stately and a network of Lakota, Dakota, Ojibwe, and Cree beaders make earrings, pendants, bracelets, and intricately detailed barrettes. The shop is open weekdays from 10am to 5:30pm. On the weekends, Stately packs up his inventory and heads to powwows and other community events.

Don't miss the outdoor murals by artists Gregg Deal and Votan Henriquez, which cover the center's eastern wall. A wooden mural on the building's Franklin Avenue façade was donated to MAIC by artist George Morrison, who created it especially for the center.

Address 1530 East Franklin Avenue, Minneapolis, MN 55404, +1 (612)879-1700, www.maicnet.org | Getting there Metro to Franklin (Blue Line) or bus 2 to Franklin Avenue East and Bloomington Avenue South | Hours Mon–Fri 7am–3pm | Tip Take in a show at All My Relations Arts, which promotes American Indian artists (1414 East Franklin Avenue, Minneapolis, MN 55404, www.allmyrelationsarts.com) and then sit back at Pow Wow Grounds coffee shop, which is in the same building.

69 Minnesota State Capitol

It's time to take another field trip

If you haven't gone inside the Minnesota State Capitol since you were in elementary school, it's time to head over to St. Paul and rediscover the place where our laws and legislation get made, especially now that a three-year, $310m restoration has the Cass Gilbert-designed building – considered one of the grandest state houses in the country – looking as shiny as a penny that's just left the mint.

There's plenty to ooh and ahh over, from the rotunda and its one-ton crystal chandelier, to the Brobdingnagian staircase lined with marble pillars, to the Governor's Reception Room, which is covered in so much gold leaf you'll be tempted to think you wandered into Versailles. But it's the unshowy changes that are in many ways more relevant and turn a visit to the Capitol into an opportunity to reflect on the less savory aspects of our state's history and the way its stories have been conveyed to the public.

When the restoration got underway, there was a rethinking about several paintings in the Reception Room and the way they represented American Indians, who have lived in what we now call Minnesota for more than 10,000 years. Two paintings were deemed either historically inaccurate or culturally insensitive and removed from the building. Two more, *Father Hennepin at the Falls of St. Anthony* and *The Treaty of Traverse des Sioux*, were relocated to the third floor, where they will be accompanied by information that helps visitors understand the historic context of the paintings.

Also, don't miss the basement Rathskeller Café, which is open during the legislative session. When the building opened in 1905, the German-themed dining hall honored the fact that Germans were the largest group of immigrants in the state. But when World War I started, the Governor ordered that the German mottos and paintings be painted over and that mottos extolling the virtues of drinking be watered down. They have since been rediscovered and restored.

Address 75 Rev. Dr. Martin Luther King Jr. Boulevard, St. Paul, MN 55155, +1 (651)296-2881, www.mnhs.org/capitol | Getting there Metro to Capitol/Rice Street (Green Line) or bus 3, 62, 67, 622 to Rice Street and University Avenue | Hours Mon–Fri 8:30am–5pm, Sat 10am–3pm, Sun 1–4pm, guided tours available | Tip It's a bit of a climb, but go see the heroic gold Quadriga (Latin for "four-horse chariot") at the base of the Capitol's dome. The sculpture is called *The Progress of the State*.

70 Mows Doors
Street art in miniature

Look down. No, lower. Right there, on the corner of that building, you'll see it – a door that's just a smidge bigger than a cell phone. The door doesn't lead anywhere, but that's beside the point. So smile and enjoy the fact that an anonymous artist, who goes by the Instagram handle Mows510 (for "mouse") has decided to turn this overlooked part of your urban landscape into an opportunity for delight. Welcome to the Mows Doors of Minneapolis.

"I make sculptures and install them in disused public places to surprise and delight people who happen upon them in their day-to-day activities," says Mows510, who started creating street art at the age of 54, first in San Francisco and now in the Twin Cities. "My art gives me the opportunity to add a bit of whimsy to public spaces while at the same time be part of a global conversation with other street artists."

Each door – they are all accompanied by a doormat – is made from resin that's poured into in silicone molds, painted, and then attached to a surface – building, tree, curb – using concrete adhesive. Some are site-specific and reflect their surrounding (a Mondrian-inspired door in the Northeast Arts District). Some add color to a blah industrial zone (a bright yellow door on an underpass). Others comment on specific cultural moments and even mourn a collective loss (that would be the purple Prince door near First Avenue).

You can find the doors by going to Mows510's Instagram, where he posts photos of them. Some locations will be obvious because they are shot with easily recognizable landmarks in the background. There's nothing stopping you from setting out to find them. Others, not so much. So keep your eyes peeled. Says Mows 510, "I chose to bring my artworks to the street level where people can engage and interact with them rather than have them be installations that are seen from a distance and never touched."

Address Look for them on street corners across the Twin Cities | **Getting there** See @Mows510 on Instagram for location information | **Hours** Unrestricted | **Tip** Mows510 has been especially active in Northeast Minneapolis. After an afternoon searching for the doors, take a break at the Indeed Brewing Company's tap room – and look for the Mows Door near the entrance (711 15th Avenue Northeast, Minneapolis, MN 55413, www.indeedbrewing.com).

71 The Museum of Russian Art

Moscow near the Mississippi

The Scandinavians and the Somalis may get all the attention, but the truth is that the Russian-speaking community is one of the oldest immigrant groups in Minnesota – many arrived as far back as the 19th century. Unfortunately, their cultural presence in the Twin Cities often went largely unnoticed.

That changed in 2002, when The Museum of Russian Art (TMORA) opened, billing itself as "the Twin Cities' window into Russian art, history, and culture." It's actually a whopper of an understatement for this gem of a museum, which boasts what is believed to be the largest privately owned collection of 19th- and 20th-century Russian realist paintings outside the borders of the former Soviet Union.

Housed in a former Congregational church built in the Spanish Colonial Revival-style – definitely a weird juxtaposition, but keep an open mind until you step inside – the galleries are perhaps the most tranquil and contemplative spaces to view art in a city known for its world-class museums. Each is a soothingly lit showcase for the paintings, photographs, and prints that bring the beauty and mystery and everyday life of this often little-known local culture to life.

The exhibitions are small enough that you can enjoy them in an hour. Themes are far-ranging: an exploration of Russian tea drinking and samovars; the representation of women in Soviet art; photographs of Jewish life in the Russian Empire. And unlike the blockbuster shows at Mia or the Walker, the intimate setting and unrushed atmosphere allow every item to tell its story. An exhibit on the legendary jewelry firm Fabergé skipped the famous eggs in favor of the picture frames, brooches, and cufflinks of the Russian royal family and their court. The Museum also sponsors lectures, concerts, and seminars.

Address 5500 Stevens Avenue South, Minneapolis, MN 55419, +1 (612)821-9045, www.tmora.org | **Getting there** Bus 18, 156 to Stevens Avenue and Diamond Lake Road | **Hours** Mon–Fri 10am–5pm, Sat 10am–4pm, Sun 1–5pm | **Tip** Three blocks over on Nicollet Avenue, treat yourself to brunch or an afternoon snack at Wise Acre Eatery, the ultimate Minneapolis field-to-fork experience (5401 Nicollet Avenue South, Minneapolis, MN 55419, www.wiseacreeatery.com).

72 Mystery of the Curator's Office

A time capsule of mid-century design

Barton Kestle was the first curator of modern art at the Minneapolis Institute of Art (Mia). Hired in 1950, he moved here from New York City, where he'd gotten a PhD from Columbia University. He was tasked with expanding the museum's collection and took to his assignment with gusto, convincing then director Richard Davis to add a photography department to the museum's encyclopedic offerings.

Kestle was a shy, scholarly guy who was known to work late into the night developing exhibits by artists such as surrealist Max Ernst. His career was off to a promising start. And then, one day in 1954, Kestle was summoned to appear before the Senate Permanent Subcommittee on Investigations in Washington, DC. He boarded a train east and was never heard from again.

The staff at Mia didn't touch his office until, in a rush to make room for another exhibit, they covered over Kestle's door. When the office was rediscovered in 2011, the curators understood immediately that it was an important cultural artifact. They turned it into one of the museum's famous period rooms.

You can see "Curator's Office" on the third floor of the museum's Target Wing. It's a time capsule of mid-century industrial design that includes Kestle's Polaroid Land Camera and Underwood typewriter, and also a filmstrip projector and a melamine plastic cup and saucer. There are even worn-down pencils in a Chock full o'Nuts coffee can and a mound of cigarette butts in a freestanding ashtray.

The room is a fascinating three-dimensional document of its time. But if you look closely, you'll start to ask questions that could challenge its authenticity. Why, for example, is there a placard crediting the room to conceptual artist Mark Dion? And how could Kestle's office be in a part of the museum that didn't exist until 2006?

Address 2400 3rd Avenue South, Minneapolis, MN 55404, +1 (888)642-2787, www.artsmia.org | Getting there Bus 11 to 3rd Avenue South and 24th Street East or bus 18 to Nicollet Avenue South and 24th Street West | Hours Tue & Wed 10am–5pm, Thu & Fri 10am–9pm, Sat 10am–5pm, Sun 11am–5pm | Tip Head over to Jasmine Deli for the excellent Vietnamese cuisine. Their bánh mì is called the best in town (2532 Nicollet Avenue, Minneapolis, MN 55404, www.jasminedelimpls.com).

73 __ Nicollet Island

Little House on the Prairie meets the big city

Sure, you probably know there's an island in the middle of the Mississippi River near downtown Minneapolis. And you probably know that it's home to both the much-loved Nicollet Island Inn and DeLaSalle High School, which has helped give the island a youthful presence since 1900.

What you probably don't know is that if you head upstream – past both the Bell of Two Friends (a gift from sister city Ibaraki, Japan), the small grove of cherry trees, the railroad tracks, and graffiti – there's a neighborhood that is so marvelously stopped in time that you can imagine you are walking through Walnut Grove with Laura Ingalls Wilder. That is until you see the skyscrapers of Minneapolis.

The fact is that the entire island is bathed in history. Before Minneapolis was a city, Nicollet Island was a sacred place for both the Dakota and Ojibwe tribes. By the turn of the 19th century, this patch of trees and water – you are never far from the rush of the current flowing toward St. Anthony Falls – was a fashionable place to live, with several Victorian mansions and limestone townhouses. The neighborhood went through boom and bust cycles before becoming the quirky gem beloved by its current residents and visitors.

Today, many of the original homes are still there, set apart from cobblestone streets by picket fences. It's the kind of neighborhood where sunflowers grow along the boulevards, and chickens cluck in their backyard coops. It's the perfect place for a walk or bike ride and a picnic in the many green spaces along the river.

For an even more unknown treat, head to the northeastern tip of the island and take the pedestrian bridge over the river to Boom Island Park, a 22.5-acre park with trails and boat docks. While Nicollet Island may feel like *Little House on the Prairie*, the experience of standing just feet above the water and wooded riverbanks is pure *Huckleberry Finn*.

Address Nicollet Island is located on the Mississippi River between downtown Minneapolis and Southeast and Northeast Main Street, Minneapolis, MN 55401 | Getting there Bus 4, 6 to East Hennepin Avenue and De La Salle Drive | Hours Nicollet Island Park and Boom Island Park are open every day of the year 6am–midnight | Tip Cross over the suspension bridge to SE Main Street and head up the stairs to Our Lady of Lourdes Catholic Church (1 Lourdes Place, Minneapolis, MN 55414, www.ourladyoflourdesmn.org). Open since 1877, it's the oldest continuously operating church in Minneapolis.

74_Norseman Distillery
Get into the spirits

In a town that has nearly reached the point of overload when it comes to microbreweries, it was only a matter of time until the spirits enthusiasts got a piece of the action. The first (legal) distillery in Minneapolis since Prohibition, Norseman Distillery uses local ingredients to produce small batches of premium vodka, gin, rum, and whiskey, not to mention a line of artisanal digestifs.

Housed in a massive warehouse amongst a grid of warehouses off East Hennepin, Norseman's cocktail room and distillery space is a Scando-industrial dream, courtesy of owner Scott Ervin, who was an architect for 20 years before he switched to mashing grain and mastering the properties of fermentation. You've got your white walls, your distressed wood and metals, your marble bar, and fancy stemware. But it's the stainless-steel stills and stacks of wooden barrels that give Norseman its soul. They remind you that the ingredients in your gin and tonic infused with creole bitters and spruce tonic – as well as a different gin seasoned with pineapple and chipotle – were made right in this very room. It's an authentic grain-to-glass experience.

All of this fancy public sipping was made possible in 2014, when Governor Mark Dayton signed a bill that allowed distilleries to sell and serve their products on-site, like a brewery taproom. Since then, the micro-distillery scene in the Twin Cities has exploded to include Tattersall Distilling, Du Nord Craft Spirits, and the 11 Wells Spirits Company, among others.

In addition to the cocktail room, Norseman also offers tours and tastings and something they call Cocktail Laboratories, better known as mixology classes. All this public outreach has clearly been good for business. When it started, Norseman's output was measured in five-gallon batches. Today, those batches are 5,000 gallons, and the cocktail room is always packed.

Address 451 Taft Street Northeast, Minneapolis, MN 55413, +1 (612)568-6299, www.norsemandistillery.com | **Getting there** Bus 25 to Stinson Boulevard and Kennedy Street Northeast or bus 61 to East Hennepin Avenue and Taft Street Northeast | **Hours** Mon–Thu 5–11pm, Fri 4pm–midnight, Sat 1pm–midnight | **Tip** After your tastings, go sober up at Black Coffee & Waffle Bar (1500 Como Avenue Southeast, Minneapolis, MN 55414, www.blackcoffeeandwaffle.com), which is open until 9pm every day. Try the apple strudel waffle, or even the savory One Bad Pig with ham and Swiss cheese.

75_ Northern Clay Center
The place for potters

"Working with clay is like playing in the dirt, but you get to make something that's functional and useful," says Amanda Dobbratz, a ceramic artist who is also the digital and marketing manager at the Northern Clay Center in Minneapolis' Seward neighborhood. "It's so immediate," she says. "You squish it, and it reacts."

Since 1990, professional artists and aspiring pinch potters experienced these tactile pleasures at one of the country's leading clay organizations ("ceramics" applies only to pieces that have been hardened with heat). Founded by a group of arts advocates that included former Second Lady Joan Mondale, the Clay Center benefited out of the gate thanks to the success of Warren MacKenzie, the internationally known potter who is based in Stillwater and who has attracted generations of students to his classes at the University of Minnesota over the course of his career. That trickle-down effect has resulted in a world-class craft organization that's uniquely devoted to a single medium.

In addition to two galleries that feature exhibitions of both emerging and established artists, many of whom will challenge your assumptions about what clay can do, the Clay Center has a sales gallery, which sells mostly functional (as in items you can use) pieces as well as sculptures.

And the classes! From wheel throwing to mosaics, there are educational opportunities for students of all ages.

The best part of a visit to the Clay Center is the chance to walk around the artists' studios, which are open to the public. If your idea of cubicles includes industrial carpeting and the manic tapping of keyboards, this delightfully messy warren of workspaces sing with the happy energy of people absorbed in their craft. It's a friendly and openhearted place that will make you want to pick up a hunk of that damp earth and see what you can make with it.

Address 2424 Franklin Avenue East, Minneapolis, MN 55406, +1 (612)339-8007, www.northernclaycenter.org | Getting there Bus 2, 67 to Franklin and 24th Avenues South | Hours Gallery Tue, Wed, Fri & Sat 10am–6pm, Thu 10am–7pm, Sun noon–4pm | Tip Visit the Textile Center, the renowned fiber arts counterpart to the Clay Center in Prospect Park (3000 University Avenue Southeast, Minneapolis, MN 55414, www.textilecentermn.org).

76_Northland Visions

Food and art of Woodland and Plains tribal nations

If you love Minnesota wild rice, you may be surprised to learn that those dark brown grains you get at the supermarket have about as much in common with authentic *manoomin* as a Pop Tart has with apple strudel. In fact, the "food that grows on water," isn't even directly related to Asian rice. When it's hand-harvested and processed using a wood fire, *manoomin* is lighter than commercial wild rice, with a smokier flavor and a more tender texture.

Unfortunately, unless you are a member of a tribal nation, it's hard to get your hands on the real deal. That is, unless you know about Northland Visions, a Minneapolis shop and gallery that specializes in the food and arts of the tribal peoples of the Woodland and Plains tribes of the Upper Midwest and Canada. The shop was opened in 1999 by Ken Bellinger, an Ojibwe man, who, after retiring from a career at 3M, saw an opening in the market for corporate gifts that specialized in authentic, nature-based foods from the northern regions. That business did well enough that the family – Ken's son, Greg, has taken over from his dad, who is now retired from his second career – decided to expand into retail and moved into the Ancient Traders Market building in what's now become part of the American Indian Cultural Corridor in Minneapolis.

In addition to wild rice, the store has a high-quality selection of other native foods, including bison jerky, chokecherry jelly, and fry bread mix. There are also traditional wooden flutes and ceremonial braids of sweetgrass, as well as sculptures and paintings in a section of the store that functions as an art gallery. And then there are what seem to be miles of beading supplies – Greg Bellinger says they are vital to the business because they bring artists and artisans to the shop, but it's heaven for anyone who enjoys the craft. Handmade artisans' wares, from pendants to barrettes, are here too – displayed in all their finely detailed glory.

Address 861 East Hennepin Avenue, Minneapolis, MN 55414, +1 (612)872-0390,
www.northlandvisions.com | Getting there Metro to Franklin (Blue Line) or bus 2 to
Franklin Avenue East and Bloomington Avenue South | Hours Mon–Sat 9am–5pm |
Tip The Minnesota Humanities Center offers a program called Bdote Field Trips,
which are day-long excursions to local sites of significance to Dakota people where you
learn about them from Dakota perspectives (987 Ivy Avenue East, St. Paul, MN 55106,
www.minnesotahumanities.org).

77__Ole Bull Statue

A forgotten Norwegian legend

Minnesota's Scandinavian heritage is so ingrained in the popular imagination that even if you've never eaten it, it's likely you know that lutefisk is a not-exactly-tasty dried whitefish that's been soaked in cold water and lye. And you've probably even heard a Sven-and-Ole joke or two.

But the truth is that there was a time not too long ago when the Swedes, Norwegians, and Danes were newcomers, and as such, treated like second-class citizens. Of those new Americans, the Norwegians were in a particularly interesting spot, given that their homeland didn't officially become independent from Sweden until 1905.

That struggle created a fierce sense of national pride and is one reason why, when a statue of Norwegian violinist Ole Bull was placed on the northern edge of Loring Park in 1897, it was such a big deal. If there's any doubt, check out the inscription on the statue's plinth, which reads, "Erected by Norwegian Americans." It's still there today, but given the city's changing demographics, the statue has fallen off the homeland pilgrimage hit list to become a quiet nap spot for the park's homeless population.

Bull was a virtuoso violinist as well as a proud proponent of Norwegian statehood. Born in 1810 in Bergen, Norway, Bull had his solo debut when he was was nine and became the director of a Norwegian musical society when he was 18. He was famous for his ability to play several notes at once on a violin that was modeled after traditional Norwegian folk fiddles.

From there, he hit the road and spent the rest of his career touring internationally, including several visits to Minnesota, where he achieved legend status with the state's Norwegian community. The bronze statue in his honor was sculpted by Jacob Fjelde, himself a Norwegian-born Minneapolitan, who created several Twin Cities landmarks, including *Hiawatha and Minnehaha* near Minnehaha Falls.

Address Harmon Place and Maple Street, Minneapolis, MN 55403 | **Getting there** Bus 4, 6, to Hennepin Avenue and Maple Street (16th Avenue) | **Hours** Unrestricted | **Tip** Head over to Hennepin to take a peek at the magnificent stained-glass windows in the Basilica of St. Mary (88 17th Street North, Minneapolis, MN 55403, www.mary.org).

78__Open Book

Make paper, read a poem, or maybe write a book

Minneapolis has been ranked the most literate city in the country for good reason. Not only do we have a tradition of independent book-stores – we're talking about you, Birchbark Books, Magers & Quinn, Wild Rumpus, Once Upon a Crime, and Mayday – we also have a healthy daily newspaper, a strong library system, and a well-educated citizenry. Literary giants like poet Robert Bly and novelists Louise Erdrich and Kate DiCamillo call Minneapolis home.

Since 2000, the city has also been home to Open Book, the first and only cultural center in the country devoted solely to the celebration of the book, from writing, to publishing, to the hands-on arts of papermaking and bookbinding. The center had three founders, who are still its primary tenants today. The Loft Literary Center (www.loft.org) offers classes and events that support writers, from beginning poets to novelists with completed manuscripts. Milkweed Editions (www.milkweed.org) is a nonprofit publisher of fiction, non-fiction, and poetry, including winners of the Nobel Prize for Literature. Minnesota Center for Book Arts (www.mnbookarts.org) is the largest center in the country devoted to the evolving form of book arts. They host exhibitions and events, rent studio equipment, and they hold classes on anything from paper marbling to origami.

Located on the eastern edge of downtown, Open Book is housed in three 19th-century commercial buildings that were gutted and combined to create gloriously sunny spaces to work and relax. The exposed brick and beams add to the chic industrial vibe as does the central staircase, which was created by artist Karen Wirth to look like a book's pages. But most importantly, there's a considered quiet that inspires creativity. Sitting in the café, you are likely to realize that those 200 pages of notes and journaling that you stuffed into a box really *could* become a memoir. Open Book has the resources to help you.

Address 1011 Washington Avenue South, MN 55415, +1 (612)215-2650, www.openbookmn.org | Getting there Bus 7, 22 to Washington and 10th Avenues South | Hours Mon–Sat 8am–8pm, Sun 10am–5pm | Tip St. Paul also has a proud literary heritage and community, which has included F. Scott Fitzgerald and Patricia Hampl. And the city's independent bookstore scene is alive and well in downtown thanks to the delightfully cluttered Subtext Books (6 West Fifth Street, St. Paul, MN 55102, www.subtextbooks.com).

79_Ordway Japanese Garden
Zen in the city

In 1955, St. Paul and Nagasaki, Japan became sister cities. It was just ten years after the US had dropped an atomic bomb on the Japanese metropolis and was the first-ever partnership between a US and Asian city.

That special relationship endures today in the stunning, although little-known, Charlotte Partridge Ordway Japanese Garden, which you get to through a passage on the north side of the Marjorie McNeely Conservatory at Como Park. The garden was a gift to St. Paul from Nagasaki and opened to the public in 1979. It was designed by Masami Matsuda, a 9th-generation landscape architect. Matsuda's design embodies the Japanese concepts of *sansui* (mountain and water) and *chisen-kaiyu* (strolling garden).

The result is a marvelous combination of nature and nurture. In keeping with Japanese gardening traditions, there are no straight paths; every curve is choreographed to open up to a unique tableau. Matsuda used pines and shrubs that are hardy in Minnesota and chose 400 tons of igneous and metaphoric rock – most of which came from a quarry in Apple Valley. Matsuda touched each to sense its energy and appropriateness for the setting.

That thoughtfulness pulses through the garden, which more than delivers on its promise to be an oasis for quiet reflection in the middle of the city. At the path's end, there's a traditional teahouse, which hosts annual tea ceremonies. This special event sells out quickly – it's not uncommon for people to have to wait a year or more to experience one. There's also an annual Japanese Lantern Lighting Festival that's held the end of August. It's based on the holiday of Oban, a Buddhist event that commemorates ancestors, whose spirits are believed to visit their relatives at this time. The celebration culminates in lighting lanterns and floating them at dusk on the garden's ponds to remember and honor those who have departed.

Address 1225 Estabrook Drive, St. Paul, MN 55103, +1 (651)487-8200, www.comozooconservatory.org | Getting there Bus 3, 83 to Como Avenue and Beulah Lane or bus 83 to Hamline Avenue and Midway Parkway | Hours Apr–Nov 10am–6pm (closed in winter), Bonsai Exhibit also open Oct–Mar 10am–4pm | Tip Enjoy a taiko drumming performance (or even take a class) at TaikoArts Midwest (2161 University Avenue West, Suite 117, St. Paul, MN 55114, www.taikoartsmidwest.org).

80_ Orfield Laboratories

Lose your voice in the quietest room in the world

If your dishwasher transitions from one wash cycle to the next without any jarring whirrs or whooshes, you can thank Steve Orfield. In the early 1980s, when the field of architecture fell on hard times, Orfield decided to take his lighting and acoustics expertise to the corporate world, where he helped clients such as Maytag, Whirlpool, and Harley Davidson discover how consumers experienced the sounds of their products.

To do that he needed a lab where he could test noises in conditions that would allow researchers to hear them so clearly they could analyze every inflection. So he took over a building in Longfellow that had been the home of Sound 80, the studio where everyone from Bob Dylan – who used it to lay down part of *Blood on the Tracks* – to Cat Stevens, Prince and Lipps Inc. (the Minneapolis band famous for the song "Funkytown") has recorded their music.

You can visit those studios today. And while it's thrilling to see a place with so much music history – the pre-digital recording devices themselves are worth the visit – the room you don't want to miss is the anechoic chamber, which, according to *Guinness World Records* is the quietest place on earth. Orfield bought it from Sunbeam – he beat out Motorola and IBM, who were also interested – when the company closed its research center.

Made of 3.3-foot-thick fiberglass acoustic wedges, the room's double walls are built with insulated steel and concrete. The floor is suspended on chicken wire. When you speak, your voice feels like it's being absorbed by a pile of towels – any sound stops almost as soon as it rolls off your tongue. It's an uncomfortable sensation, but according to Orfield, nothing compared to being left alone inside the chamber. That's when all you can hear is the noise of your body and internal organs doing their thing, an experience he says makes most visitors stir crazy.

Address 2709 East 25th Street, Minneapolis, MN 55406, +1 (612)721-2455,
www.orfieldlabs.com | Getting there Bus 9,7 to East 25th Street and 27th Avenue South |
Hours By appointment Mon–Fri, email info@orfieldlabs.com, tours cost $100/per person
and are led by Orfield himself | Tip Birchwood Café nearby is known for its farm-fresh,
organic brunches. Try the savory waffle (3311 East 25th Street, Minneapolis, MN 55406,
www.birchwoodcafe.com).

81 Payne Avenue

Main Street meets global market

Thanks to the railroads that trace the path of now-underground Phalen Creek, St. Paul's East Side has long been separated from the rest of the city. Set on the hills overlooking downtown and the Mississippi, it can feel like its own world, which is ironic because it's also known as a place that embraces new Americans. Early immigrants were originally drawn to the area for jobs at the Hamm's Brewery and a sandpaper company from Two Harbors that would later become a familiar business called 3M.

Since the late 1800s, Payne Avenue has been the economic center of the East Side. And even though the companies that provided so much stability to the neighborhood have now closed, the street has – after struggles personified by a former strip joint called, er, *The Payne Reliever* – figured out how to stay vibrant, not by becoming the latest outpost for Subway and Taco Bell but by doubling down on its identity as a cross between a small town American Main Street and a global market. Walking down the southern section of Payne, you'll see the offices for Hmong TV Network, Supermercado La Palma, and AAA All City Vacuum.

You'll also happen upon some of the city's cleverest, relatively new restaurants. Cook St. Paul (www.cookstp.com) serves American contemporary diner breakfasts and lunches, as well as Korean dinners on Friday nights. Tongue in Cheek (www.tongueincheek.biz) uses animal products that are "raised or caught in a humane & sustainable manner" for anything from roasted bone marrow Rockefeller to octopus scampi. And Brunson's Pub (www.brunsonspub.com), which is named for Benjamin Brunson, an original St. Paul land surveyor, updates the comforting standards, from bacon mac & cheese, to black eyed pea hummus, to maple soy chicken wings with chipotle ranch dip. Happily, these foodie establishments have enhanced and not overridden their historic street and neighborhood.

Address Payne Avenue, St. Paul, MN 55101 | Getting there By car: from downtown St. Paul, take I-94 E to Mounds Boulevard. Turn left on Mounds Boulevard and then take a left on 7th Avenue East. Take a right on Payne and drive just under a mile. | Tip Make a side trip to check out the old-fashioned meat market and ready-made pizzas and pasta sauces at Morelli's (535 Tedesco Street at Payne Avenue, Minneapolis, MN 55101, www.morellismarket.com), an Italian food shop and liquor store that's been in business since 1915.

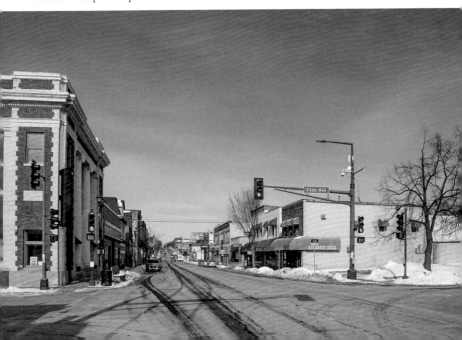

82 __ Prince's Chanhassen
The place he called home

Prince may have spent his formative years in North Minneapolis, his home as an adult was in Chanhassen, the western suburb where it's still possible to see cornfields rising up between the subdivisions. At first blush, this Anywhere USA community seems like an odd fit for such an idiosyncratic artist. But Chanhassen's remote location and Minnesota's nice locals seemed to offer Prince both the physical seclusion and emotional space he needed.

He first moved there in the early 1980s, to a house – now gone – at 9401 Kiowa Trail. He later relocated to 7141 Galpin Boulevard, where the leafy stretch of land between Lake Anne and Lake Lucy included a windmill decorated with butterflies. The house was razed in 2006, but you can still see the gatehouse that used to guard the property.

When he died in 2016, Prince was living at Paisley Park, the recording and performance mega-complex on Audubon Road, which fans already knew as the site of his legendary impromptu late night shows. It's now a museum, where you can go on guided tours that celebrate his creative process and get a peek into his personal life, including the tiny living room where he used to watch the Timberwolves and the Lynx play on TV.

Kind of like a mix between Graceland and the Rock & Roll Hall of Fame, Paisley Park's tour starts with a moment of reflection underneath Prince's ashes, which are suspended in an urn that's a replica of Paisley Park itself. From there, it's a nonstop celebration of Prince's artistic genius. In Studio A, you'll see the LinnDrum machine that defined his '80s sound, including "When Doves Cry." There are costumes galore, music scores, and the original motorcycle from *Purple Rain*. And there's the Hohner Telecaster knockoff with the leopard pick guard that was his signature and was featured in the video for "1999," which was filmed at the Minneapolis Armory in downtown.

Address Paisley Park, 7801 Audubon Road, Chanhassen, MN 55317, www.officialpaisleypark.com | **Getting there** From Minneapolis, take MN-62 W to US-212 W to MN-5. Keep going west until Audubon Road. | **Hours** Mon & Tue 9am–5pm, Thu 9am–7pm, Fri 9am–9pm, Sat 9am–11pm, Sun 10am–5pm. Purchase tickets online in advance. | **Tip** Prince was a regular at the Chanhassen Cinema, which now features a 40-foot mural in his honor (570 Market Street, Chanhassen, MN 55317, www.paisleypark.com).

83 Purcell-Cutts House

A Prairie School masterpiece

One of the most masterful examples of the Prairie School of architecture in the United States, this East Isles home was designed in 1913 by William Gray Purcell and George Grant Elmslie for Purcell and his family. Following the Prairie School philosophy – the architects were students of Louis Sullivan and colleagues of Frank Lloyd Wright – the architecture followed the then-radical idea that a building should reflect its natural surroundings. Purcell wanted an open floor plan because he felt that, unlike the formal, room-stuffed homes of his childhood, spaces with multiple uses were more progressive and embodied modern values.

That informal spirit infuses the home – the stained-glass windows that frame the front door even say "Peek A Boo." But make no mistake: the Purcell-Cutts house is also aesthetically exquisite and well engineered. Drawers were built into beds and walls to reduce clutter. A bedroom sink was hidden in a closet and rolled out on casters when needed. And a button on the hallway floor between the kitchen and dining room opened and closed a pocket door, so that the maid could step on it as she walked to the dining room to serve meals, trapping the heat and smells on the other side.

It's also an intentionally tranquil retreat from the stresses of the world, which at the time the house was designed, was working up to World War I. From the soothing color palette of gold, umber, and mauve, to the wraparound windows that fill the house with light, and the stenciled patterns that are used instead of molding, the house is a celebration of the belief that beauty nourishes the human soul. Simply standing in the living room and taking in all the carefully considered details will lower your blood pressure. Now owned by the Minneapolis Institute of Art, the Purcell-Cutts house is a masterwork that promotes the value of simplicity in the modern world.

Address 2328 Lake Place, Minneapolis, MN 55405, +1 (612)870-3000, www.collections.artsmia.org/info/purcell-cutts-house | Getting there Bus 6, 12, to Hennepin Avenue and 24th Street West | Hours Open the second weekend of each month for tours. Purchase tickets at www.artsmia.org | Tip If you like historic homes, pay a visit to the Ard Godfrey House, which is the oldest surviving frame home in the Twin Cities (28 University Avenue Southeast, Minneapolis, MN 55414, www.minneapolisparks.org/parks__destinations).

84__Quatrefoil Library

When a book collection comes out of the closet

In the mid-1970s, David Irwin and his partner Dick Hewetson began collecting gay-themed books, storing them in the linen closet of their condo on Grand Avenue in St. Paul and loaning them to friends. As their collection expanded, it became clear that it was time for their informal library to come out of the closet – literally.

Founded in 1986, Quatrefoil was the second LGBTQIA+-focused lending library to open in the United States. Irwin chose the name to honor the 1950 novel by James Barr, which was one of the first modern novels to portray homosexuality in a positive light – and to have a happy ending. At a time when publicly expressing your sexuality could put you in physical danger, Irwin and Hewetson wanted to create a welcoming space where the LGBTQIA+ community could go and safely learn more about themselves.

That mission turned out to be so needed that both the library's collections and membership mushroomed to the point where it's moved twice to accommodate over 15,000 books, all of which are available for checkout, and 7,000 DVDs. They also have an extensive collection of LGBTQIA+ periodicals, CDs, and even LPs. More importantly, the welcoming spirit that Irwin, who passed away in 2009, and Hewetson envisioned infuses the current location on Lake Street in Minneapolis.

More than just a lending library, Quatrefoil's collections are also documents of LGBTQIA+ history and changing societal attitudes about homosexuality and gender identity. On the library's west wall, a glassed bookcase houses first editions and rare books, including *Lawrence of Arabia*, the lesbian novel *The Well of Loneliness* by Radclyffe Hall, and Alfred Kinsey's *Sexual Behavior of the Human Male* and *Sexual Behavior of the Human Female*. Taking in the titles and the variety of meanings embedded in them is a deeply moving reminder of the long road Quatrefoil's community has walked.

Address 1220 East Lake Street, Minneapolis, MN 55407, +1 (612)729-2453, www.qlibrary.org | **Getting there** Bus 21 to 12th Avenue South and East Lake Street | **Hours** Mon–Fri 7–9pm, Sat & Sun 10am–5pm | **Tip** Take a walk in Loring Park (www.minneapolisparks.com) in downtown Minneapolis, the site of the annual PRIDE celebration.

85 Riverside Plaza

Eyesore or landmark?

Designed by acclaimed Minnesota architect Ralph Rapson – he was the mastermind of the original Guthrie Theater – this massive apartment complex in the Cedar Riverside neighborhood on the West Bank of the University of Minnesota is the Twin Cities' most famous, although not universally adored, example of brutalist architecture. Originally called Cedar Square West, the development's design was heavily influenced by French architect Le Courbusier, who favored rugged materials (the French word for "raw" is *brut*, hence "brutalist") and a straightforward aesthetic that eschewed the pomp and flourishes of more traditional Beaux Arts buildings.

When they completed the development in 1973, Rapson and the city planners hoped – with its prime location between the University of Minnesota and the downtown area – that it would become a community where people of varying incomes lived together in a new urban neighborhood built in a dilapidated area. That optimism was telecast to the greater world when Mary Richards, the fictional heroine of *The Mary Tyler Moore Show*, moved there from her Kenwood apartment for seasons six and seven.

While the planners' egalitarian vision was never fully realized, Riverside Plaza does play an often underappreciated role in our cities' civic life. In a time of skyrocketing rents, it has long been a stalwart of affordable housing, especially for new Americans. Today, the complex has over 4,000 residents – many from Somalia and other East African countries – who have transformed Cedar Riverside into a dynamic, multicultural neighborhood.

After showing signs of age, the buildings themselves, which were added to the National Register of Historic Places in 2010, have also been transformed with a $65 million renovation that, along with improving energy efficiency, added a new layer of paint to the primary colored panels that give the complex its flair.

Address 1600 South 6th Street, Minneapolis, MN 55454 | Getting there Metro to West Bank (Green Line) or bus 22 to Cedar Avenue South and 6th Street South | Hours Unrestricted from the outside | Tip Chow down at Dilla's (1813 Riverside Avenue, Minneapolis, MN 55454, www.dillasethiopianrestaurant.com), the neighborhood's most popular Ethiopian restaurant. Or scout out where Union Hmong Kitchen is doing its current pop-up residency. Offerings include a Kamayan Feast, a traditional communal-style Filipino meal (locations vary, www.unionkitchenmn.com).

86 Riverview Theater
Midcentury moviegoing

The first movie shown at the Riverview Theater when it opened in 1948 was *June Bride*, starring Bette Davis and Robert Montgomery. But the most important year even today is 1956, when the theater's owners, brothers Bill and Sidney Volk, decided to invest $50,000 to redecorate the lobby in an ultramodern style that looked more like a living room than a generic public space. It even had a separate television lounge to celebrate the importance of what was then a groundbreaking new medium. In an era filled with grand movie theaters, the Riverview, which was the sister of the long-gone Camden, Nile, and Terrace theaters, was a standout, complete with marble coffee tables, imported Italian lamps, and even potted plants. The concessions stand included stools and a counter, so patrons could relax and enjoy their refreshments.

You can't sit at the counter anymore, but the rest of the Riverview's 1950s decor is pretty much unchanged, including that TV-lounge, a ladies bathroom with kitty-patterned-wallpaper, and much of the original midcentury modern furniture. The theater itself, while not as much of a time capsule as the lobby, is still a blast from the past, with a stadium-style layout that holds over 700 people – the seats, thankfully, are new – and a backlit proscenium stage. And while the Riverview's days as a first-run movie palace are over, it has achieved cult status as a second-run theater that people flock to from all over the metro area. The theater also serves what one critic claimed is the best popcorn in town. In fact, the salty snack is so beloved that people in the neighborhood often get it to go.

The Riverview is also known for special annual events, including a wildly popular *The Sound of Music* Singalong and a Hitchcock festival. They also broadcast live sporting events and other public occasions that appeal to its left-leaning community, including a live broadcast of Barack Obama's first inauguration.

Address 3800 42nd Avenue South, Minneapolis, MN 55406, +1 (612)729-7369, www.riverviewtheater.com | Getting there Bus 23, 9 to 38th Street East and 42nd Avenue South | Hours Visit the website for show times. | Tip The Grandview 1 & 2 is St. Paul's most charming neighborhood movie theater, known for its beautiful art deco marquis (1830 Grand Avenue, St. Paul, MN 55105, www.manntheatres.com).

87 Roller Garden

Stayin' alive for more than 70 years

This St. Louis Park mainstay got its start in 1930 as the Pastime Arena, a horseback riding school founded by prominent Minneapolis businessmen who wanted a nationally-known venue for their horse shows and equestrian contests. It was the only permanent structure for horse events and polo matches in the Twin Cities besides the pavilion at the Minnesota State Fair and was definitely a chic place to see and be seen.

By the 1940s, new owners flooded half of the arena each winter and took out ads touting "…figure and general skating. Competent Instructions, Good natural ice. Music by Electric Organ." By 1943, flooring was installed for roller skating, much to the dismay of the neighbors, who sued because they worried about the noise. (Half of the arena was still reserved for riding, which makes you wonder why there were no complaints about any neighs and whinnies.)

Little did those neighbors know that, after a stint as Minneapolis' first indoor tennis center, this building would be synonymous with music and roller skating for generations of tweens. You may be among those who were equal parts thrilled and traumatized during the Snowball, where the girls lined up on one side of the arena and the boys on the other, hearts pounding when a whistle blew to indicate it was time to "couples skate" under the neon flashes of a disco ball.

Today, fans don't seem to mind that the Roller Garden is slightly more threadbare than it was when K.C. and the Sunshine Band, Donna Summer, and Kool & the Gang topped the charts. Kids still flirt and struggle to keep their balance when they hold hands or skate backwards. And then there are the adults, many of whom are part of the sober crowd (the most mind-altering drink served at Roller Garden is Mountain Dew) who swizzle, toe tap, and basket weave around the rink, lost in funkadelic reveries and rolling to the beat.

Address 5622 West Lake Street, St. Louis Park, MN 55416, +1 (952)929-5518, www.rollergarden.com | **Getting there** Bus 17, 667 to Minnetonka Boulevard and Vernon Avenue | **Hours** Tue & Fri 5–11pm, Wed 5–8pm, Thu 8:30–11pm, Sat 11am–4pm & 7–10pm, Sun 10am–noon & 12:30–3:30pm; also available for private rental | **Tip** Take your free-wheeling skating skills outside or rent a bike to enjoy the Minneapolis Chain of Lakes Regional Park, which takes you around lakes, past beaches, through gardens, and past many other scenic points along the way (www.minneapolisparks.org/parks__destinations).

88_ St. Paul Corner Drug

An Rx for community wellbeing

Since it opened in 1922, this neighborhood general store and pharmacy is truly the kind of place where everyone knows your name, not to mention what you're on. Kidding (and privacy laws) aside, in a time of big-box drug stores and long waits at urgent care centers, the opportunity to give patients personalized attention is why John Hoeschen purchased this St. Paul business in 1997. Being a community pharmacist – he and his family live two blocks away – has allowed Hoeschen and his staff to move beyond managing customers' prescriptions to attending to other factors that can impact a person's well-being: nutrition and navigating the healthcare and insurance systems. It's an approach that breeds loyalty. People who grew up shopping there may have moved away, but they stop by when they come to town.

St. Paul Corner Drug is equally adored for its soda fountain, which serves malts, shakes, ice cream cones, sundaes, and floats. Soda water was once thought to have health benefits, which is why soda fountains were popular at drug stores. Pharmacists made the drinks and mixed in other ingredients, drawing on their experience making prescriptions. ("Rx" actually stands for "recipe.")

Once soda pop went mainstream, the popularity of soda fountains began to wane. But they live on in our imagination, which is why it's so nostalgic when St. Paul Corner Drug's fountain workers whip up bygones of the soda jerk era, including phosphates, which are flavored sodas that are made with acid phosphate instead of citric acid. The acid phosphate boosts the flavor with a pleasant sourness and makes your tongue tingle – cherry is the classic flavor, although they're also available in lime, chocolate, and orange. You can also take part in a morning ritual that has stayed the same since St. Paul Corner Drug first opened its door: a cup of coffee still costs only five cents.

Address 240 Snelling Avenue South, St. Paul, MN 55105, +1 (651)698-8859, www.stpaulcornerdrug.com | Getting there Bus 84, 70 to Snelling and St. Clair Avenues | Hours Mon–Fri 8:30am–7:30pm, Sat 8:30am–5pm | Tip Grab a sandwich from the St. Paul Cheese Shop (1573 Grand Avenue, St. Paul, MN 55105, www.stpaulcheeseshop.com) and enjoy a picnic on the grounds of Macalester College.

89__St. Paul Curling Club

Brush up on all things bonspiel

If you're like most people, your knowledge of the winter sport of curling is limited to what you've seen at the Winter Olympics. You know it's played on ice, and that it seems a little bit like shuffleboard, except that the players scramble alongside 42-pound granite stones, furiously brushing the ice with devices that look like mops.

Most Minnesotans don't know, however, that the largest curling club in the country is on Selby Avenue in St. Paul. Founded in 1912, the St. Paul Curling Club (SPCC) is not only an institution in this subculture of all sports subcultures, the cedar-paneled upstairs lounge is also a lively neighborhood bar where the beer flows and visitors treat themselves to self-serve Jägermeister shots.

The roots of the club stretch back to the late 1800s, when the Scottish sport was played on the frozen Mississippi; SPCC's first competition was held on the river near Navy Island on Christmas Day 1885. Today, the club hosts regular game play as well as *bonspiels*, or tournaments that draw teams from across the country and Canada. It's a lively scene – kind of like a cross between a hockey game and a bowling tournament – but make no mistake: fans are surprisingly intense about the action taking place on the eight sheets of ice, and the players are as focused on their tasks as chess masters. Unlike most sports, however, this one has strict rules of etiquette. Opponents greet each other with a handshake and compliment each other's shots. Winners usually buy a round of drinks for the losers. In curling, manners matter.

That camaraderie may account for the sport's increasing popularity in the Twin Cities and across Minnesota. There are over 20 curling clubs throughout the state, with four in the metro area alone. SPCC's events are open to the public. You can also take lessons and even rent the club out for private parties, with or without curling instruction, although weekend and evening times are limited.

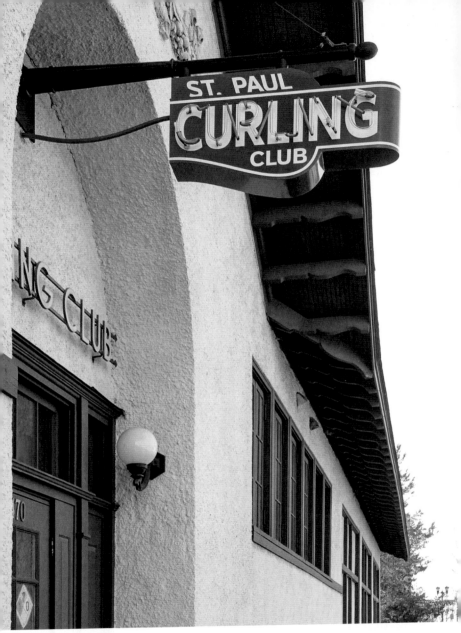

Address 470 Selby Avenue, St. Paul, MN 55102, +1 (651)224-7408,
www.stpaulcurlingclub.org | Getting there Bus 21 to Selby Avenue and Mackubin Street
or bus 65 to Dale Street North and Selby Avenue | Hours Daily 4–11pm, from October
through May. Lessons and special events by appointment. | Tip One block west on Selby,
the St. Paul outpost of Revival serves the most rave-worthy fried chicken in town (525 Selby
Avenue, St. Paul, MN 55102, www.revivalfriedchicken.com).

90 The Salt Cave
Take the halotherapy cure

In 2011, Scott Wertkin and Jenni Dorfsman were on vacation in Florida when they happened upon a TV program touting the benefits of halotherapy, an alternative health treatment that's been known to help people who suffer from asthma, allergies, COPD, and other respiratory issues. Discovered in 1843 by a Polish physician who noticed that salt mine workers were immune to the kinds of lung diseases that plagued other miners, salt therapy is based on the belief that intensive exposure to air that's infused with microparticles of pharmaceutical-grade salt helps eliminate mucus buildup in the lungs and sinuses.

Both Wertkin and Dorfsman had undergone sinus surgery and were intrigued. But when they returned home to Minnesota, they discovered the closest halotherapy spa was in Chicago. So they set to work researching how to design and build a therapeutic salt cave. And that's how a business was born.

Located in Minneapolis' Tangletown neighborhood, The Salt Cave is actually two separate rooms walled with pink bricks of Himalayan crystal salt that's imported from Pakistan. Designed and built from scratch by Dorfsman and Wertkin, both rooms have floors that are covered in salt that's as soft as flour and walls that are backlit so that the translucent bricks glow with a womb-like warmth, a feeling that intensifies when you sit back in one of the zero-gravity lounge chairs. As the lights dim and the soundtrack of crashing waves overtakes low sounds of a halogenerator pumping the salt into the air, your shoulders loosen and release all the stress they normally hold. Your nostrils tingle just the tiniest bit as your sinuses start to drain. You feel like you're floating on a cloud.

And then, before you know it, 45 minutes have passed, and you begin to come back to real life. You had assumed that The Salt Cave's claim of helping relieve stress was just a marketing gimmick. You were so wrong.

Address 4811 Nicollet Avenue, Minneapolis, MN 55419, +1 (612)567-2587,
www.saltcaveminnesota.com | Getting there Bus 11, 18, 46 to Nicollet Avenue South
and 48th Street West or 49th Street West | Hours Tue–Fri 10am–7pm, Sat 10am–5pm,
Sun noon–5pm | Tip Continue the wellness experience with a visit to the homeopathic
and herbal remedy experts at Present Moment (3546 Grand Avenue South, Minneapolis,
MN 55408, www.presentmoment.com).

91 Schmidt Artist Lofts

Where creativity is on tap

For over a century, St. Paul was home to some of the most important breweries in the US. When Jacob Schmidt's original operation on the bluff above what is now the Bruce Vento Nature Sanctuary burned to the ground in 1899, he moved upriver to West 7th Street and bought the Cave Brewery, which he expanded into a 16-acre complex that is so stately and sprawling it could almost be mistaken for a Gothic castle. Over the years, many brands, including Schmidt, Grain Belt, Old Style, Blatz, Pig's Eye Pilsner, and Pete's Wicked Ale were brewed at this site. After it closed for good in 2002, the brewery was converted into an ethanol processing plant.

Then the bottling house and the brewery were renovated in 2012 and turned into the Schmidt Artist Lofts, where people who are engaged in creative pursuits can rent affordable studio and living spaces to pursue their endeavors. The soaring ceilings and limestone walls feel both of the moment and steeped in the past, as do other industrial touches, such as mash tubs and some of the brewery's original signage.

The building is open to the public twice a year in spring and fall during the St. Paul Art Crawl, when residents sell and display their art in the on-site galleries. Explore Minnesota, the state's tourism organization, stops there on its St. Paul Brewing History bus tour. But while it's worth marking your calendar to take a peek inside, you'll also enjoy just walking the grounds, too. If you are lucky, Phil Gagne, the brewery's last brew master, will be in his office in the well house and will show you his collection of memorabilia: beer cans, steins, and the brewer's seniority cards, which showed who had priority in bidding for jobs and vacation time. Gagne's many stories are bittersweet reminders that while the buildings have gotten a second chance, many workers' lives were forever changed when this part of St. Paul went dark.

Address 900 West Seventh Street, St. Paul, MN 55102, +1 (651)451-5921, www.schmidtartistlofts.com | Getting there Bus 74 to 7th Street West and Palace Avenue | Hours Unrestricted from the outside. Check website for Art Crawl information. | Tip Next door in an old Schmidt warehouse, Keg and Case West 7th Market is a foodie nirvana in the tradition of San Francisco's Ferry Building, with chef-driven restaurants and an array of gourmet shops (928 West Seventh Street, St. Paul, MN 55102, www.kegandcase.com). You can also treat yourself to the extremely pure brewing water sold in a vending machine on the brewery's 7th Street façade.

92__ The Shoe Tree
An urban mystery

For decades, students at the University of Minnesota have taken pairs of shoes – most often sneakers, but Doc Martens, flip-flops, and soccer cleats have also been spotted – tied the laces together, and flung them off the Washington Avenue Bridge, which links the campus's East and West Banks over the Mississippi. The lucky shoes land on the branches of a tree that towers several stories high on the Minneapolis side of the river's edge.

Some shoes have the dates of the flinging inscribed with a Sharpie on their toecaps. Others include messages across their outer soles: "Thanks for proving every1 right," one reads, mysteriously.

Why these shoes are here, dangling like clumps of dirty grapes, is anyone's guess. But when the *StarTribune* tried to get to the bottom of the mystery, the newspaper of record came up empty handed. Perhaps, they surmised, it's a ritual to mark passing exams or losing one's virginity, or confirming you are actually going to graduate. It could be all of the above.

Or not. The University says that the tradition is for alumni, who toss the shoes they wore to walk across the enormous campus when they were undergrads. Whatever the reason, all that's known for certain is that this tradition has been going on for over 45 years, which corresponds to when the Washington Avenue Bridge was moved and rebuilt in 1965 to connect to the West Bank. Did someone have a little too much to drink at Palmer's and, in a moment of collegiate exuberance, toss their shoes over the bridge on their way back to their dorm?

That we don't really know is, of course, part of the appeal. Standing on the bridge's upper deck, you'll be amazed that so many Nikes, Keds, and Adidas were able to snag a branch mid-flight. Those that didn't make it are scattered on the ground alongside the shoes whose laces, after years of being worn thin by the rain and snow, just couldn't hold on any longer.

Address The West Bank of the Washington Avenue Bridge, Minneapolis, MN 55455 | Getting there Metro to West Bank (Green Line) or bus 122 to 19th South and Washington Avenues South | Hours Unrestricted | Tip On the other end of the Washington Avenue Bridge, check out the elevators in Coffman Memorial Union, the site of an iconic photograph of The Replacements by local photographer Daniel Corrigan (300 Washington Avenue Southeast, Minneapolis, MN 55455, www.sua.umn.edu).

93__Skyway Secrets

Take a walk in a human Habitrail

Many urban planners despise the Minneapolis and St. Paul skyway systems. Not only do these "human Habitrails" suck the life out of downtown sidewalk culture, they also detach us from the essence of our Minnesotaness, which is inextricably tied to extreme weather. North Loop entrepreneur Eric Dayton feels the skyways have such a negative impact on our cities that he started the "Skyway Avoidance Society" as a way to nudge citizens and city leaders to take a hard look at why our downtown cores can feel so lifeless. And yet, until our downtowns get people back on the streets, the skyways are important pedestrian arteries in each city. If you aren't ready to avoid them, there are plenty to explore, especially in Minneapolis, which has miles of skyways that allow you to get from the Convention Center to within a block of the Mississippi. So set aside an afternoon, with the intention that you are going to try and get from, say, Target Center to US Bank Stadium using only these suspended sidewalks, and see what you find.

While you're on your urban treasure hunt, take the time to check out the Wells Fargo History Museum on the skyway level of the Wells Fargo Center at 90 South Seventh Street. An historic look into both the origins of the mega-bank and the way mail and people traveled during the stagecoach era, it's a truly interesting – and interactive – blast into the past. You can have your photo printed onto currency (and learn about the legislation that made doing so illegal in 1862 after a man named Spencer Clark put his mug on some bills). And you can sit in a stagecoach and watch as the landscape changes from prairie to snowy woods to mountains, imagining all the bumps on the trails. The stagecoach is so cramped you can't help from reflecting that perhaps "coach class" in modern air travel is named after these less than luxurious early modes of transportation.

Address In Minneapolis visit www.skywaymyway.com, in St. Paul visit stpaul.skywaymyway.com | **Getting there** May vary but in general Mon–Fri 6:30am–10pm, Sat 9:30am–8pm, Sun noon–6pm | **Tip** The Thrivent Financial Collection of Religious Art (625 Fourth Avenue South, Minneapolis, MN 55415, www.thrivent.com/offers/art.html) is on the skyway level of the Thrivent Financial building and has more than 1,100 objects, including Medieval choir books and works by Rembrandt and Picasso.

94 The Southern Theater

Decrepit glory in Seven Corners

Opened in 1910 as a theater specializing in Swedish drama and weekend silent-film matinees for kids, The Southern Theater has gone through many phases, from an "adults-only" movie theater to an antiques shop. But while other historic venues in town have updated themselves with extensive and beautiful buff and polish jobs, The Southern is so proud of its wrinkles that it's eschewed any fillers or injections that could relieve its worry lines.

In fact, the stage of the 165-seat theater is the definition of crumbling glory, with a proscenium arch that's missing chunks of plaster and seems not to have had a paint job since the place opened. It's so beautifully decrepit that if it were outdoors you'd be tempted to think you'd stumbled into an ancient ruin.

After some ups and downs (it was a garage and warehouse in the early 1950s) The Southern got back to its roots as a performing space when the Guthrie Theater leased it to use as a second stage in 1975. When they left, community activists fought to prevent the building from being razed and turned into a motel.

That same community spirit is alive and well today. As a venue for performance companies without a bricks-and-mortar location, The Southern acts as a loving aunt to many of the region's upstart theater companies, who, after being evaluated by a panel that decides each season's lineup, get to use the theater for free.

That doesn't mean The Southern doesn't have any regulars. Every Saturday night, the theater is home to BALLS Cabaret, the long-running (they claim the longest anywhere on earth) weekly midnight cabaret that's the brainchild of singer, writer, and producer Leslie Ball. An experimental stage for artists of any discipline and level of experience, it's a relaxed and supportive venue where anyone from a standup comedian to an a cappella group can experience the magic of performing live.

Address 1420 South Washington Avenue, Minneapolis, MN 55454, +1 (612)326-1811, www.southerntheater.org | Getting there Metro to West Bank (Green Line) or bus 7, 22 to Cedar and Washington Avenues | Hours See website for performance schedule | Tip Enjoy a pre-show beer or cider from the exhaustive tap list at Republic (221 Cedar Avenue South, Minneapolis, MN 55454, www.republicmn.com).

95 Steamboat Minnehaha

Resurrected from the depths of Lake Minnetonka

Yes, many of us know that the Twin Cities streetcar line was once the envy of the country. But did you realize that in the early 1900s, middle-class shopkeepers who commuted to the downtown area and the servants who worked at the estates on Lake Minnetonka traveled between their jobs and homes on steamboats that were an extension of the Twin Cities Rapid Transit (TCRT) trolley line? In fact, they were so popular that by 1921 ridership topped 220,000.

Sadly, that era of scenic public transportation came to an end shortly thereafter, when the roads around Lake Minnetonka's windy bays improved and automobiles became more affordable. By 1926, TCRT cancelled the service and got rid of the fleet by – and this is not a joke – sinking them in the deeper parts of the lake near Big Island. That's where the lovely *Minnehaha* stayed for 54 years, until she was rediscovered by an underwater construction crew.

As with the streetcar enthusiasts who restored and stewarded the vestiges of our overland trolley system back to the streets, volunteers gave the *Minnehaha* a second life thanks to their diligence and hard work, spending six years replacing rotted wood, caning the seats, and locating and installing a vintage steam engine (now powered by diesel). The result is a delightful respite from the whoops and roars of ski boats and wet bikes on a lake that's known more for booze cruises than history tours.

The *Minnehaha* operates throughout the summer and fall (the foliage tours are especially popular). You can travel between Excelsior and Wayzata, with a lunchtime layover in the middle. Or you can choose a guided history tour. "Victorian Gems, Cottage Treasures" takes you past Big Island and Minnetonka Beach and is a peaceful way not only to enjoy Lake Minnetonka but also learn about what it was like before all the hotel-sized mansions took over its shores.

Address 37 Water Street, Excelsior, MN 55331, +1 (952)474-2115, www.steamboatminnehaha.org | **Getting there** Take Highway 7 to the 2nd Street / Old Log Way exit | **Hours** Regular tours operate on Sat & Sun and holidays during the summer and fall. | **Tip** Excelsior is the Twin Cities' most charming suburb, and Water Street is lined with restaurants and high-end home shops. Leipold's Gifts & Antiques (239 Water Street, Excelsior, MN 55331) is a throwback junk store, where you can lose yourself in the stacks of antique books and postcards.

96__StevenBe
Express your inner glitter knitter

When Steven Berg decided to call time on a corporate career in the fashion industry that included a stint as a vice president at Perry Ellis, he asked his mom what he should do. Her advice? "Sell some yarn."

Berg listened to his momma – and then some! If your idea of a yarn shop has something to do with earth tones and women who think a wild afternoon involves debating the right way to do popcorn stitch, it's time to head over to Chicago Avenue to meet this self-proclaimed "Glitter Knitter" at his 6,000-square-foot fiber arts palace. There's a crystal chandelier, as befits Berg's status as nationally known stitching royalty. And there are acolytes, although truthfully they seem to be more in the service of their own creative muses – one has been known to sport a Princess Leia-style wig made from violet and aqua balls of yarn – than their fiber arts boss/impresario. The scene feels as uninhibited as a play date with Rainbow Brite, only raunchier.

With his flamboyant and irreverent sensibility, Berg is at the forefront of a movement that has rescued knitting, felting, and other fiber arts from their utilitarian and earnest roots. There are patterns for men's bikinis, aka banana hammocks, and an item called an "organ grindr," which you'll have to see for yourself. If you're in the mood to fashion a pair of "swants," (otherwise known as a sweater worn as pants), no one here will stop you. Truly, anything goes.

None of this freewheeling artistry would matter, of course, if StevenBe didn't deliver the goods. Berg has one of the best yarn assortments in the country: miles of skeins in colors that range from an ombré pink fuchsia to grays so dense you'll think you're staring at a Seattle sky. And they stock hard-to-find brands, including a plump superchunky from British yarnery Mrs Moon that feels as soft as baby cashmere even though it's a merino-alpaca blend. Weavers will be similarly delighted with their options. Cast on!

Address 3448 Chicago Avenue South, Minneapolis, MN 55407, +1 (612)259-7525, www.stevenbe.com | **Getting there** Bus 5 to Chicago Avenue South and 35th Street East or bus 23 to Chicago Avenue South and 38th Street East | **Hours** Mon, Wed & Fri 11am–6pm, Tue & Thu 11am–7pm, Sat 11am–4pm, Sun 11am–4pm | **Tip** Play ping-pong and browse around the Third Place Gallery (3730 Chicago Avenue, Minneapolis, MN 55407, www.wingyounghuie.com), which is an arts-incubator/gallery/urban living room. Photographer Wing Young Huie inaugurated his gallery space in 2011 and hosts monthly art events.

97　The Stone Arch Bridge

The most romantic walk in town

The Stone Arch Bridge wasn't created to provide romantics with a Hollywood backdrop for their love-soaked dates. In fact, this National Register of Historic Places landmark, which spans the Mississippi River just below St. Anthony Falls, got its start in 1883 when railroad magnate James J. Hill built the 2,100-foot-long stone behemoth so his trains could cross into downtown Minneapolis.

At the time, the haters didn't hold back their opinions of "Jim Hill's folly." A bridge with 23 arches set above the violent froth on the downside of the falls? Impossible! But when Hill's crew finished the project in less than two years, even the cranks had to admit the bridge was not just an engineering marvel: it was staggeringly beautiful.

It is perhaps even more beautiful today. Owned by the state since 1992, the Stone Arch Bridge is now used by pedestrians and bikers, who enjoy it in every season, not just as a way to get from downtown to the St. Anthony Falls Historic District, but also to take in the brute power of the falls from a perch that feels so close to the action it makes your pulse race.

Crossing the river on the diagonal, the bridge curves westward toward the shore by Mill Ruins Park. It's a glorious place to be late on a summer evening as the heat dissolves and the light drains from the sky. On one side, the skyscrapers showcase the power of industry. On the other, the leafy St. Anthony Falls Heritage Trail tugs at your spirit. The combination of urban grit and nature is intoxicating, which is why it's the perfect place to take that special person who you hope will be inspired to, well, take things to the next level.

To increase your chances, finish your walk on the side of the bridge that meets SE Main Street, a cobblestone road that's the prettiest thoroughfare in town. You can even hire a horse-drawn carriage if you are feeling so inclined.

Address West River Parkway across from Mill City Museum, Minneapolis, MN 55401, www.minneapolisparks.org | Getting there Bus 7, 22 to Washington Avenue South and Park Avenue | Hours Daily 6am–10pm | Tip Continue the romance with a drink or dinner on the crazy-charming patio of the Aster Café (125 Southeast, Main Street, Minneapolis, MN 55414, www.astercafe.com).

98 Swede Hollow Park

A walk on the wild side

One of the oldest and poorest settlements in St. Paul, the immigrant neighborhood known as Swede Hollow, was located below Dayton's Bluff, literally underneath the Hamm's Brewery, where many residents worked. The extended Hamm family lived high on the bluff in a Queen Anne brick mansion and several other homes. For over 100 years, the community down in the ravine never had electricity, and plumbing was limited to outhouses built on stilts above Phalen Creek, which flowed into the Mississippi.

The sanitation became so worrisome that in 1956, the city decided that conditions had rendered the neighborhood a health hazard and, after evicting every resident, burned it to the ground.

That tragic history hangs in the air as you descend past the former brewery, which after falling into disrepair, is now home to both 11 Wells Distillery and Flat Earth Brewing Co. But as the landscape deepens into what's now Swede Hollow Park, it's impossible not to be swept up in the tranquility of this hidden patch of St. Paul. The buzz and honks of the traffic on Payne Avenue and East 7th Street seem like they've been absorbed by the woods that line both sides of the ravine, replaced by the burble of flowing water, the whistles and trills of birds, and the very enthusiastic peeps of the frogs who now call the park home.

It's an easy walk down to the Seventh Street Improvement Arches, which mark the park's southern entrance. A historic and civil engineering landmark, the highway bridge was built in 1883 and is known for its spiral design, which when seen from underneath the arch makes it look like the project was built on a slant. On your way back to the park's northern entrance, look into the woods to spot foundations and other signs of the homes that exist only in memory. Then get your heart pumping on the long set of stairs to an historic marker and scenic overlook.

Address Payne Avenue and Beaumont Street Southeast, St. Paul, MN 55130, www.stpaul.gov/facilities/swede-hollow-park | **Getting there** Bus 64 to Payne and Minnehaha Avenues. Finding Swede Hollow by car can be tricky. To get to the park's main entrance, drive northeast on Payne. Look for a tiny metal sign near Beaumont Street Southeast. Turn right on Beaumont and then left on Drewry Street, which is a dead end. | **Hours** Unrestricted | **Tip** Located on the other side of the Arches, the Bruce Vento Nature Sanctuary is a spring-fed wetlands that also is an important site for Native Americans (4th Street East, St. Paul, MN 55106, www.nps.gov/miss/planyourvisit/ventosanctuary.htm).

99 Tao Café & Herbery

A throwback to health food's salad days

Sure, juicing is so much the rage these days that a glass containing the liquid of fresh-pressed apple, kale, ginger, spinach, romaine, cucumber, and lemon is almost ho-hum. But don't let the fact that healthy eating has gone mainstream stop you from visiting this trailblazing East Isles cafe, which has been talking up the virtues of organic produce and ancient grains since 1968.

The cafe's quiet and sun-drenched vibe is a throwback to that time, complete with the very friendly and chill counter workers, who have been known to not only take their sweet time with an order in an effort to get it exactly right but also to sigh and refuse customers any service until said customers get off their cell phones and rebalance their energy. Sure, it's a little judgy, but take a deep breath: the larger point about the loss of civility and manners in a preoccupied and always-connected world *is* spot on.

Once you go with the way Tao flows, you will be delighted by simple but thoughtfully prepared dishes, from bone beef broth spiced with turmeric and ginger to chana masala wraps to bowls of quinoa topped with beets, sweet potatoes, a poached egg and a swirl of lemon vinaigrette. They also whip up tonics infused with superfoods, including cacao, coconut milk, and herbal formulas.

Tao is also known for its cozy, well-stocked natural health store. If you're worried about wheezing through allergy season, the Tao staff will instruct you on all manner of home cures, including adding obscure herbs to your soup stock. Who knew? Sore joints, PMS, headaches, insomnia – whatever ails you, Tao has a supplement or herb that may help you feel better. And the teas! Let's just say the selection goes well beyond chamomile. There's also a nice assortment of health books, including cookbooks, and classes on anything from how the quantum mechanics of the laws of attraction govern our thoughts and intentions to a creative cooking camp for kids.

Address 2200 Hennepin Avenue South, Minneapolis, MN 55405, +1 (612)377-4630, www.taonaturalfoods.com | Getting there Bus 2, 6 to Hennepin Avenue South and 22nd Street West | Hours Mon−Sat 8am−9pm, Sun 10am−8pm | Tip Two blocks down Hennepin, Via's Vintage specializes in clothing, jewelry, and accessories from the 1920s to the 1980s (2408 Hennepin Avenue South, Minneapolis, MN 55405, www.viasvintage.com).

100__Tiny Diner

A little restaurant with very big ideas

Not many restaurateurs would see a former gas station and envision an upscale diner for the Minneapolis Powderhorn neighborhood *and*a working laboratory for permaculture, an agricultural philosophy that recreates natural ecosystems to grow plants sustainably without repeatedly tilling the soil. Then again, not many restaurateurs have the start-up bug and off-the-canvas vision of Kim Bartmann, the Wisconsin native and visionary behind Cafe Barbette, Bryant Lake Bowl, and Red Stag Supperclub, among others.

In addition to a creative kitchen that switches its menu every month to pay homage to the diner cuisine of different towns across America – the Chicago menu, for example, shows a lot of love to the hot dog – Tiny Diner practices urban farming literally in its backyard. Not only is there a garden where Tiny Diner Farm, which is down the street on 42nd Avenue, grows edible flowers and vegetables, the restaurant also has a small grove of mesabi cherry trees and a rainwater catchment system, where rain that hits the roof is stored and reused without entering the sewer system.

In fact, the entire place practically sings with the happy notes of nature and commerce serenading each other. The massive patio is covered with a solar array, which, in addition to generating energy, casts a pleasing blue shade that keeps diners cool even in the August swelter. A willow thicket fort provides shelter for kids. A rooftop bee colony and pollinator-friendly plants ensure that Tiny Diner is doing its part to save this threatened species.

And if that's not enough, there's a Thursday farmer's market and classes, which are held at both the diner and Tiny Diner Farm. Whether you want to learn about growing plants from seed, mulching, straw bale gardening or preserving herbs and fungi, Tiny Diner is committed to making sure that your breakfast, lunch, and dinner are more than just meals.

Address 1024 East 38th Street, Minneapolis, MN 55407, +1 (612)767-3322, www.tinydiner.com | Getting there Bus 23 to East 38th Street and 10th Avenue South | Hours Daily 7am–10pm | Tip Powderhorn Park (3400 15th Avenue South, Minneapolis, MN 55407, www.minneapolisparks.org) has tennis and basketball courts, a wading pool, and a lake stocked every year with crappies, sunfish, and catfish. In winter, there's a skating rink and sledding hill – watch for the annual Art Sled Rally (www.artsledrally.com).

101 __ Tool Library

Access over ownership

When Thomas Ebert moved to Minneapolis after 13 years of living in Portland, he dreamed of importing a service that had taken hold in the eco-savvy Pacific Northwest. The result is the Northeast Minneapolis Tool Library (NEMTL), and its younger sibling, the St. Paul Tool Library. A community resource that allows members, who pay an annual fee, to borrow anything from a caulk gun, to a cable drain auger, to a sewing machine, it's also a workshop where hobbyists, makers, and DIYers can share tips while they work on the mitre saw or woodworking lathe.

Ebert, the library's director who co-founded NEMTL with Andover native Zach Wefel, sees the NEMTL as an environmentally conscious way for people to save money on needless purchases. "Every garage on the block doesn't need to have the same equipment," says Ebert, presumably referring not just to lawnmowers and leaf blowers, but also tillers, circular saws, hedge trimmers, and the chainsaw apron chaps that you really ought to wear when you borrow that chainsaw.

The library is a happy, industrious place, where on any given afternoon people line up to get their hands on a power washer, use the library's in-house table saw, or even browse through the assortment of manuals and instruction books. Eventually, the NEMTL team hopes to expand to locations across the state.

NEMTL is located in the Thorp Building in Northeast Minneapolis. A massive warren of studios, galleries, and offices for painters, lawyers, cocktail artisans, bodybuilders, and many others, the building started its life in 1902 as a fire door factory. During World War II, it was turned into a secret manufacturer for bombs and military equipment on par with the Manhattan Project. You can still see two guard towers that were once used by the FBI and the CIA to protect the place. Today, it's known more for being the birthplace of Art-A-Whirl, the neighborhood's freewheeling open studio tour.

Address 1620 Central Avenue Northeast, Suite 126, Minneapolis, MN 55413, +1 (612)440-8665, www.nemtl.org | **Getting there** Bus 10 to Central and 18th Avenues Northeast or bus 30 to Central Avenue and Broadway Street Northeast | **Hours** Wed & Thu 4–7pm, Sat 10am–4pm | **Tip** Feel free to explore the art studios and notice the endless nooks and crannies of the Thorp Building itself, which is home to dozens of artists, artisans, and craftspeople (1618–1620 Central Avenue Northeast, Minneapolis, MN 55413, www.bohmcre.com/thorp.htm).

102 Underground at the Walker

When modern art goes subterranean

Since 1988, the Sculpture Gardenhas been the most well known attraction in the glorious Minneapolis park system. In June 2017, this already beautiful gem emerged from over a year of tender care and is now shinier and more beautiful than ever. New trees have been planted. WiFi has been installed. The iconic *Spoonbridge and Cherry* sculpture has been repainted. And that's not all: the garden has also added 18 new artworks, including Katharina Fritsch's *Hahn/Cock*, a 13-foot-tall, bright blue rooster on a massive parapet that towers over the garden's northern edge. Standing next to it makes you feel small, which is, after all, kind of the point.

There's also a new 30-minute Art Loop, a free walking path that connects you, the walker, to the adjoining hillside, giving visitors easier access to American artist and MacArthur fellow James Turrell's *Sky Pesher*, 2005.Basically a bunker hidden in the hill next to Groveland Terrace, it's long been a secret pleasure to Sculpture Garden visitors, many of whom have discovered it by accident and were enchanted by the way Turrell uses light and optical illusions to redefine our relationship to the world above us.

From the outside, the cement entrance feels more like a storage garage or tornado shelter. But step inside, and your eyes go immediately to a white ceiling that curves just slightly before opening up to the sky. If you visit right before sunrise or sunset, you'll get to experience how Turrell, through computer-controlled sensors, combines natural and artificial light to create an optical effect that makes the space feel like it's vanishing as the sky comes down to greet you. It's an astonishing sensation. But if you can't get to *Sky Pesher* at those exact moments, don't worry. At any time of day it's a truly unique space where you can just sit back and watch the clouds go by as if they are art in a frame.

Address 725 Vineland Place, Minneapolis, MN 55403, +1 (612)375-7600, www.walkerart.org | Getting there Bus 4, 6, to Hennepin Avenue and Vineland Place | Hours Tue, Wed & Sun 11am–5pm, Thu 11am–9pm, Fri & Sat 11am–6pm | Tip Try the Daisy Contemporary cocktail at Esker Grove, the museum's acclaimed restaurant (723 Vineland Place, Minneapolis, MN 55403, www.eskergrove.com).

103 Union Depot

A building with stories to share

This massive neo-classical beauty in St. Paul's Lowertown neighborhood was designed in 1913, but its history dates back to the original St. Paul Union Depot Company, which was made up of nine railroads, including James J. Hill's Great Northern Railroad. After fires destroyed the first two depots, Hill decided that the state's capital (not to mention his company) needed a station that could both handle more traffic and make a statement.

That grand vision ended when the last passenger train left the station on April 30, 1971, and the National Railroad Passenger Corporation (better known as Amtrak) was launched the next day, running its Twin Cities operations out of Minneapolis. For the next forty years, the Depot's waiting room and concourse were shuttered, while a revolving door of restaurants tried to make a go of it in the historic Head House.

Then, in 2010, the Ramsey County Regional Railroad Authority, which had purchased the building, got to work restoring the depot in the hopes that, with Metro Transit's new Green line, which now has its terminus at the Depot's steps, the building would become a transportation hub and a new center of activity. But while Amtrak and regional and national bus lines now use the Depot, the overall feeling is more like a museum than, say, Grand Central Terminal.

Which actually makes it a fascinating place to explore, thanks to the free audio walking tours you can listen to on your smartphone. If you have any interest in history, transportation, architecture, or public art, this building has stories to share. Literally. Check out the brass speakers embedded in stone cubes and benches. That's Amateur Intelligence Radio (AIR), an interactive radio station that uses artificial intelligence and information provided by commuters to broadcast what's going on in the building. There's even a speaker that's hidden behind a door. Can you find it?

Address 214 4th Street East, St. Paul, MN 55101, +1 (651)202-2700, www.uniondepot.org | Getting there Metro (Green Line) or bus 3, 16 to Union Depot and Gate A 1 or bus 63 to Kellogg Boulevard and Broadway Street | Hours Unrestricted | Tip Explore hip and historic Lowertown, especially the St. Paul Farmers' Market, which is open April–October, and Saturdays only during the winter (290 East 5th Street, St. Paul, MN 55101, www.stpaulfarmersmarket.com).

104_ Universe of Light at MOA
Say goodnight to the Great Indoors

Over 40 million people visit the Mall of America (MOA) each year, which is more than the populations of Iowa, North Dakota, South Dakota, and Canada combined. So it's a safe bet that with all the publicity those attendance numbers generate, there's not that much left for anyone to discover at our world-famous homage to the "Great Indoors", that's not related to a really great sale.

That is unless you find yourself at Nickelodeon Universe 30 minutes before the mall closes. Silent are the overlapping soundtracks of 50 different pop songs and shrieks that rise and fall with the dips and turns of the log chute all day long. Instead, the whir of wheels against roller coaster tracks becomes white noise. Custodians joke as they bag up trash, and an employee at The LEGO Store spritzes disinfectant and wipes down the play tables. A lone mall jogger, probably dreaming of his bed at the Radisson Blu, gets in one last lap around the second level. And then you hear the announcements for "Universe of Light."

This light-and-music show takes place in the space between Hard Rock Café and the Backyardigans Swing-Along ride near the mall's south entrance. You'll be encouraged to head to the second or third level for the best viewing. If you have young children, though, you'll want to stay on the first floor.

You'll know that the show is about to start when the fog machines cloud the park – that's so that you'll be able to see the lasers. And then… the lights go and (recorded) music swells. The singer's voice contains all the inspiration and hope and big feelings of a Disney heroine. She assures you that "We're always here for you," and given that the lyrics also include a mention of a roller coaster ride, you understand she's referring to the MOA. After nine minutes of choreographed strobes and smoke plumes and lasers shooting off eight different disco balls, you'll be glad you stayed late at the mall.

Address 60 East Broadway, Bloomington, MN 55425, +1 (952)883-8800, www.mallofamerica.com | **Getting there** Metro to Mall of America (Blue Line), see the website for driving directions | **Hours** Mon–Sat 9:30pm, Sun 7pm. The show doesn't run in late August and early September due to the late sunsets. | **Tip** At SEA Life Minnesota Aquarium at Mall of America you can watch the shark feedings, Tue–Thu 1pm. Jellyfish are fed every Friday and Saturday at 2:30pm (www.visitsealife.com/minnesota).

105 __ University Grove
A Mecca of mid-century modern homes

Tucked between the farm and golf course on the University of Minnesota's St. Paul Campus, the land for this relatively unknown neighborhood was originally set aside in the 1920s when, after seeing a community for the employees of Stanford University, University Vice President William Middlebrook persuaded his colleagues that a similar community would be a great recruiting tool for potential faculty and administrators. His vision turned out to be so compelling that plans for the football field originally slated for that location were moved to make way for the new neighborhood just across the St. Paul border in Falcon Heights.

Central to Middlebrook's vision was that the land in University Grove would be owned by the university – residents would own their homes and lease the land for a nominal fee. This unique ownership structure, which is still in place today, helped to control development and costs as well as maintain architectural integrity and character. Each of the 103 homes in the Grove was, per the community's rules, designed by an architect.

And what architects! The first house, a 1929 English Tudor on Folwell Street, was by William Ingemann, who was also the architect of Stillwater's Lowell Inn. But while there's no shortage of mint-condition Tudors, colonials, and prairie-style ramblers, it's the bounty of mid-century modern homes that is the neighborhood's calling card today. From Bauhaus to international style, the Grove is a showcase of Minnesota modern architects, including Ralph Rapson, who designed the original Guthrie Theater and Riverside Plaza, and Winston and Elizabeth Close, who lived in the neighborhood and designed 14 homes there. Today, university employees still have priority when homes go on the market here, which has helped retain its bookish vibe. So if an astrophysicist asks to borrow your lawnmower, you know why.

Address University Grove is off Cleveland Avenue on the University of Minnesota's St. Paul Campus, ugrove.umn.edu | **Getting there** By car: take 35W to the Larpenteur Avenue Exit and head east to Coffman, where you will turn south. The U of M's free Campus Circulator makes a stop in the Grove that connects you to both the St. Paul and Minneapolis campuses. | **Hours** Unrestricted | **Tip** Explore the neighborhood of St. Anthony Park, especially the St. Anthony Park Branch Library, which was funded by a Carnegie Corporation grant in 1914 (2245 Como Avenue, St. Paul, MN 55108, www.sppl.org) and the Old Muskego Church, a wooden structure that was the first Norwegian church built in the US in 1844 (1425 Grantham Street, St. Paul, MN 55108).

106_ Victory Memorial Drive

A ride through the days of World War I

The largest war memorial in the Twin Cities, Victory Memorial Drive was officially dedicated in 1921 – a time when the American automobile industry was one of the world's greatest success stories. Which means that while people certainly would have strolled underneath the allée of elms that stood in two perfectly spaced rows on the grassy park that runs through the center of the street, it would have been a particular thrill to take a Model-T or Studebaker out for a spin along the memorial's 3.8-miles of parkway that traces the northwestern corner of Minneapolis.

The Drive was the brainchild of parks advocate Charles Loring and legendary park planner Theodore Wirth. Both were inspired by the City Beautiful movement, an urban planning philosophy that sought to import the aesthetics of European cities to the United States in the hopes that Americans – many of whom were moving to cities from rural areas – would rethink their conviction that urban areas were dirty, congested, and unsafe.

While Victory Memorial Drive is definitely not the Champs-Élysées – the lovingly-maintained craftsman and Tudor bungalows, while charming, don't have that Belle Époque majesty – both streets are monuments to their nations' armies. Each of the 568 trees on Victory Memorial Drive represents one of the 568 servicemen and nurses from Hennepin County who died in World War I. Their names appear on bronze plaques that are placed in front of those trees. (The original elms have been replaced, unfortunately thanks to both our harsh climate and Dutch elm disease, so the canopy Wirth and Loring envisioned is still in progress.) Midway through the park there's a memorial plaza with a flagpole and monuments to those who died. Each year on Veteran's Day (11/11) at 11:11am, the sun lines up with that flagpole and casts a shadow over the marker for Armistice Day – as poetic a tribute as you can get.

Address The Drive goes between the northern edge of Theodore Wirth Parkway and Webber Park. | Getting there Drive north on Theodore Wirth Parkway. To start at Webber Park, take I-94 to the Dowling Avenue North exit (228) and follow signs to Webber Park. | Hours Unrestricted | Tip At the plaza, head west on Lake Drive to downtown Robbinsdale for the early dinner seating of the tasting menu at Travail Kitchen & Amusements. If you aren't up for the complicated online ticketing process or the high price tag, check out their sister restaurant, Pig Ate My Pizza (4124 West Broadway Avenue, Robbinsdale, MN 55422, www.pigatemypizza.com).

107 __ The Weisman's Flophouse
Eavesdropping is encouraged

Perched on a hill overlooking the Mississippi on the University of Minnesota's East Bank, the Frederick R. Weisman Museum looks like a medieval fortress that woke up one morning and decided it wanted to reinvent itself as a carnival funhouse. Better known as the Weisman, the building was designed by renowned architect Frank Gehry, with unconventional angles and stainless-steel skin offering a playful wink – not to mention a blaze of reflected sunshine – to the U's otherwise grand, academic institution-style buildings.

Inside, the Weisman has over 25,000 works of art in its permanent collection, which is especially strong in American modernism, ceramics, Mimbres pottery, and Korean furniture. There's much to see, but a standout is the mixed media *The Pedicord Apts.* Created by the late Edward Kienholz and Nancy Reddin Kienholz, who built it from scraps of a deserted residential hotel in Spokane, WA, the three-dimensional exhibit is an eerie recreation of a rooming house lobby and hallway, complete with cheap paneling, threadbare carpet, an ashtray with real cigarette butts, and a fake plant.

It's a depressing and claustrophobic … and a captivating way to travel back to what feels like a 1950s last resort. If you lean against the apartment doors, a sensor triggers recordings of the lives the Kienholzs imagined could have taken place behind them. There's the sad whine of a phone off the hook – a sound that's almost a relic when heard from the perspective of the age of texting – the raised voices of a man and woman fighting, the frustrated desperation of a dog barking. It's uncomfortable enough that part of you wants to escape back to the aesthetic pleasures of the museum's bright white minimalism, which certainly holds even more treasures to explore. But if you're like most people, you'll decide to stay and listen even more closely in the hope that this fake version of reality will eventually tell you its many secrets.

Address 333 East River Road, Minneapolis, MN 55455, +1 (612)625-9494, www.wam.umn.edu | Getting there Metro to East Bank (Green Line) or bus 2 to Washington Avenue and Coffman Union | Hours Tue, Thu & Fri 10am–5pm, Wed 10am–8pm, Sat & Sun 11am–5pm | Tip Take in the sweeping views of the Mississippi and downtown Minneapolis with a walk or bike on the upper deck of the Washington Avenue Bridge.

108 West Broadway Avenue

An urban renaissance

With above average rates of violent crime, a foreclosure crisis spurred by the recession, and a stubborn achievement gap in its public schools, it's tempting to feel as though the greater Twin Cities has turned its back on North Minneapolis, an historic neighborhood that was once the soul of a vibrant Jewish community. Those challenges only intensified when a 2011 tornado ravaged the Jordan neighborhood. George Floyd's murder in the summer of 2020 was yet another traumatic blow to this predominately Black neighborhood.

But make no mistake. This overlooked pocket of our city is a hotspot for grassroots creativity and community spirit. That spark is at its most electric on West Broadway Avenue, which has, in recent years, seen a boomlet of culinary and artistic advances.

Start your afternoon with lunch at the delightful and mouth-watering Breaking Bread Cafe (1210 West Broadway Avenue, Minneapolis, MN 55411, www.breakingbreadfoods.com). In a neighborhood that's saturated with fast-food outposts, this homey sit-down restaurant serves up tangy jerk shrimp, plates of grits, and citrus kale salads. The food is great, as is the mission to serve as a community gathering spot, create new jobs for local residents, and inspire other entrepreneurs to invest in the neighborhood.

For dessert, head across the street to Cookie Cart (1119 West Broadway Avenue, Minneapolis, MN 55411, www.cookiecart.org). Started in 1988 by Sister Jean Thuerauf as a way for neighborhood teenagers to get off the streets and into jobs, the shop buzzes with the energy of young adults as they scoop dough and take orders. Try the Chicago Butter cookie, a shortbread that was created by an intern who had studied at the local Le Cordon Blue College of Culinary Arts.

From there, check out the murals and public art from the gas station that's covered in paintings of stylized boom boxes to the neighboring trompe l'oeil-meets-mosaic stylings at 1108 West Broadway.

Address West Broadway Avenue, Minneapolis, MN 55411 | Getting there Bus 14, 30 to West Broadway and Fremont Avenues North or bus 5 to West Broadway and Emerson Avenues North | Hours Unrestricted | Tip At the end of every July, the FLOW Northside Arts Crawl is a self-guided tour of not just murals, but pop-up galleries, drum sessions, parades, and more (www.flownorthside.org).

109 __ Willie's American Guitars

A shop that strikes a chord

They may have been famous for some of the most natural harmonies in show business, but Phil and Don Everly – better known as the Everly Brothers – had the kind of issues you'd expect when you spend every waking moment with your sibling. Those resentments boiled over into a whopper of a fight, which led to a smashed guitar and a decade of estrangement.

That guitar's case – which, apparently, contains a few slivers of said guitar – sits on the floor of a room stocked with beautifully restored Martins, Taylors, and Gibsons in the acoustic section of Willie's American Guitars, an unimposing storefront on Cleveland Avenue in St. Paul. Several rock and roll legends have wanted to buy it, but the store's owner, Nate Westgor – Willie was his stage name when he was part of the Chicago music scene in the 1980s – says it's too good for his business' mojo to sell.

Westgor clearly understands a thing or two about nurturing that kind of magic. When he moved to the Twin Cities and opened Willie's in 1989, he drew on the relationships he'd built repairing and selling mostly-used guitars to some of the world's most famous musicians, including Bruce Springsteen and The Rolling Stones. Today, Westgor is the guy to call when musical acts – Billie Joel, Neil Young, Eric Clapton – stop in the Twin Cities. Even Nicolas Sarkozy, the former president of France, has purchased a guitar from Willie's extensive selection of vintage and collectible instruments.

While it's unlikely you'll spot Keith Richards tuning a Telecaster to open-G – Westgor usually hand-delivers the goods to his stratospherically famous customers – you might spot Lyle Lovett or even Sheryl Crow browsing the inventory. But beyond possible star sighting, a visit to Willie's will put you in the company of the local guitar players and music lovers whose gigs and garage practices produce the soundtracks of our streets.

Address 254 Cleveland Avenue South, St. Paul, MN 55105, +1 (651)699-1913,
www.williesguitars.com | Getting there Bus 87, 134 to Cleveland and St. Clair Avenues |
Hours Mon–Thu 11am–7pm, Fri 11am–6pm, Sat 11am–5pm | Tip Now that you've
got an instrument, get inspired at Hymie's Vintage Records (3820 East Lake Street,
Minneapolis, MN 55406, www.hymiesrecords.com).

110__ Witch's Hat Water Tower
Dorothy not included

Prospect Park was born in 1884, when real estate speculator Louis Menage petitioned the Minneapolis City Council to accept two plots of land he wanted to develop. Because of the area's hilly topography, the neighborhood was laid out with winding streets instead of a grid, which, along with a bounty of impressive Queen Anne and Colonial Revival-style houses, accounts for much of Prospect Park's non-cookie-cutter charm. That eclectic vibe is enhanced by a variety of Tudor Revivals, English-style cottages, craftsman-style bungalows, and on Bedford Street, a small Frank Lloyd Wright-designed home, which is partially visible from the street.

Then as now, the neighborhood is, thanks to its position between the Mississippi River, the University of Minnesota, and Interstate 94, largely cut off from the rest of the city. As a result, Prospect Park has always had a fierce sense of community pride and activist spirit, including the city's first neighborhood association and the Prospect Park Study Club, a women's group that was founded in 1896 to promote intellectual activities for its members.

Popular with professors and students from the nearby university campus, who rent out apartments in the area's duplexes and fourplexes, parts of Prospect Park appear as shabby as a college town, which gives the historic district a sense of authenticity. The neighbor-hood landmark is its water tower, dubbed the Witch's Hat for its green, cone-shaped roof. Built in 1913 after extensive lobbying by the neighborhood association in an effort to improve local water pressure, it was erected on what's now known as Tower Hill Park, the highest natural land mass in Minneapolis. The views from the park are terrific, but the water tower's observation deck is open only one day a year – the Friday after Memorial Day – when the Pratt neighborhood hosts its annual Ice Cream Social. There are always lines, so plan accordingly.

Address 55 Malcolm Avenue Southeast, Minneapolis, MN 55414 | Getting there Metro to Prospect Park (Green Line) or bus 16 to University and Malcolm Avenues Southeast | Hours Daily 6am–midnight | Tip Across University Avenue, see for yourself why Surly Brewing Company has become the superstar that it is (520 Malcolm Avenue Southeast, Minneapolis, MN 55414, www.surlybrewing.com).

111 Zoran Mojsilov Sculptures

When a wrestler becomes an artist

As a teenager growing up in Belgrade, Yugoslavia, Zoran Mojsilov discovered a passion for Greco-Roman wrestling. While he stopped competing in his mid-20s, his appreciation for the sport's aggressive muscularity – not to mention the discipline needed to train – endures today in the massive public sculptures he's installed across the Twin Cities since he moved here in 1986.

Mojsilov spent his 62nd birthday at a public celebration at Can Can Wonderland (see ch. 13), where a masseuse walked on his back while playing the accordion (he was wearing bikini underwear). So if your taste in art tends toward subtle, look elsewhere because Mojsilov's sculptures definitely announce themselves, often sexually, even though they are made from materials – wood, stone, metal – that honor our natural and manmade surroundings.

You can find Mojsilov's sculptures all over town. And once you acquaint yourself with his artistic language – he often uses rebar as a rope to lasso the stone – you'll be able to spot them in unexpected places. Get started on your Mojsilov exploration at 77 13th Avenue NE by the Mississippi in Northeast Minneapolis, where you'll find what looks like an industrial reinterpretation of Stonehenge. The surroundings are unmanicured, which make the park feel like a pop-up shop, except that logic tells you bulldozers were involved in its making. Pieces of it are set to move across the road to a new playground.

From there, head up to the Dowling exit off I-94 to the Camden Gateway project on Lyndale Avenue North and take a seat on the sculpture ironically named *Lazy Boy*. Next, head south to Kenwood School (2013 Penn Avenue South) to see a stone poem and rain garden he created with author Louise Erdrich. Visit his website to find more of his work around the Twin Cities.

Address 77 13th Avenue Northeast, Minneapolis, MN 55413 (outdoor studio),
www.zoranmojsilov.com | **Getting there** Bus 30 to Broadway and Marshall Streets
Northeast or bus 11 to 2nd Street and 13th Avenue Northeast | **Hours** Unrestricted |
Tip Conclude your tour with a meal or music show at Icehouse (2528 Nicollet Avenue
South, Minneapolis, MN 55404, www.icehousempls.com), which has a courtyard created
by Mojsilov. Then head to Target Field to see his fountain, Curveball (1 Twins Way,
Minneapolis, MN 55403).

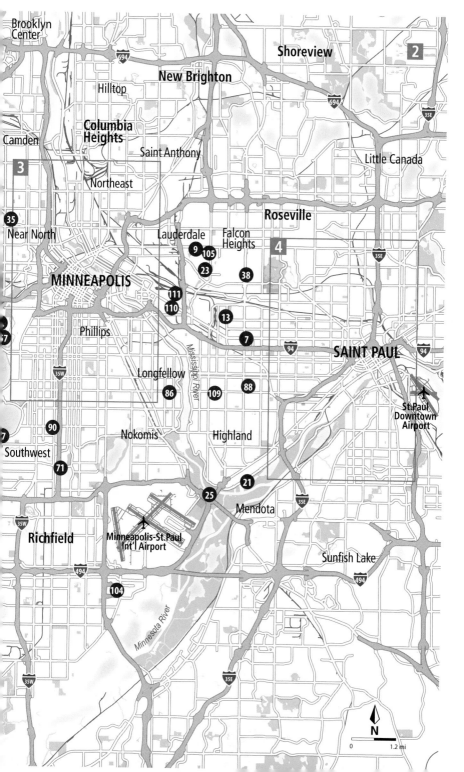

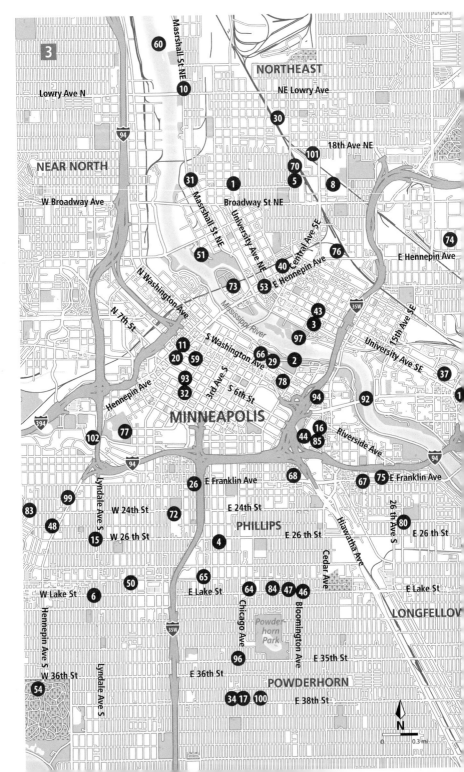

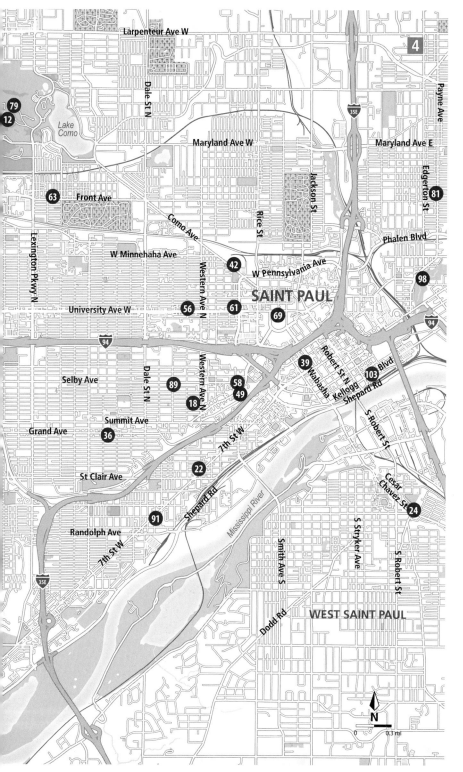

Amy Bizzarri, Susie Inverso
111 Places in Chicago
That You Must Not Miss
ISBN 978-3-7408-0156-4

Michelle Madden,
Janet McMillan
111 Places in Milwaukee
That You Must Not Miss
ISBN 978-3-7408-0491-6

Sandra Gurvis, Mitch Geiser
111 Places in Columbus
That You Must Not Miss
ISBN 978-3-7408-0600-2

Floriana Petersen, Steve Werney
111 Places in San Francisco
That You Must Not Miss
ISBN 978-3-95451-609-4

Laurel Moglen, Julia Posey,
Lyudmila Zotova
111 Places in Los Angeles
That You Must Not Miss
ISBN 978-3-95451-884-5

Heather Kapplow,
Kim Windyka, Alyssa Wood
111 Places in Boston
That You Must Not Miss
ISBN 978-3-7408-0894-5

Jo-Anne Elikann
111 Places in New York
That You Must Not Miss
ISBN 978-3-95451-052-8

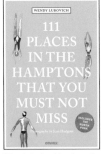

Wendy Lubovich, Jean Hodgens
111 Places in the Hamptons
That You Must Not Miss
ISBN 978-3-7408-0751-1

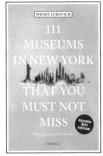

Wendy Lubovich, Ed Lefkowicz
111 Museums in New York
That You Must Not Miss
ISBN 978-3-7408-0379-7

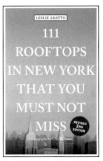

Leslie Adatto, Clay Williams
111 Rooftops in New York
That You Must Not Miss
ISBN 978-3-7408-0495-4

John Major, Ed Lefkowicz
111 Places in Brooklyn
That You Must Not Miss
ISBN 978-3-7408-0380-3

Kevin C. Fitzpatrick, Joe Conzo
111 Places in the Bronx
That You Must Not Miss
ISBN 978-3-7408-0492-3

Joe DiStefano, Clay Williams
111 Places in Queens
That You Must Not Miss
ISBN 978-3-7408-0020-8

Andréa Seiger, John Dean
111 Places in Washington
That You Must Not Miss
ISBN 978-3-7408-0258-5

Allison Robicelli, John Dean
111 Places in Baltimore
That You Must Not Miss
ISBN 978-3-7408-0158-8

Cristyle Egitto, Jakob Takos
111 Places in Palm Beach
That You Must Not Miss
ISBN 978-3-7408-0897-6

Gordon Streisand
111 Places in Miami and the
Keys That You Must Not Miss
ISBN 978-3-95451-644-5

Travis Swann Taylor
111 Places in Atlanta
That You Must Not Miss
ISBN 978-3-7408-0747-4

Dana DuTerroil, Joni Fincham,
Daniel Jackson
111 Places in Houston
That You Must Not Miss
ISBN 978-3-7408-0896-9

Kelsey Roslin, Nick Yeager,
Jesse Pitzler
111 Places in Austin
That You Must Not Miss
ISBN 978-3-7408-0748-1

Katrina Nattress, Jason Quigley
111 Places in Portland
That You Must Not Miss
ISBN 978-3-7408-0750-4

Dave Doroghy, Graeme Menzies
111 Places in Vancouver
That You Must Not Miss
ISBN 978-3-7408-0494-7

Anita Mai Genua,
Clare Davenport,
Elizabeth Lenell Davies
111 Places in Toronto
That You Must Not Miss
ISBN 978-3-7408-0257-8

Benjamin Haas, Leonie Friedrich
111 Places in Buenos Aires
That You Must Not Miss
ISBN 978-3-7408-0260-8

Beate C. Kirchner,
Jorge Vasconcellos
111 Places in Rio de Janeiro
That You Must Not Miss
ISBN 978-3-7408-0262-2

Christoph Hein, Sabine Hein
111 Places in Singapore
That You Shouldn't Miss
ISBN 978-3-7408-0382-7

Kai Oidtmann
111 Places in Iceland
That You Shouldn't Miss
ISBN 978-3-7408-0030-7

Acknowledgements

First and foremost, infinite thanks to my parents Robert Larsen and Sheila Morgan for modeling civic pride and the importance of always giving back to our community. I'd also like to offer a shout out to my dear friend Angela Erdrich for her late night texts and emails filled with ideas for this project and our enthusiastic field trips across the Twin Cities. If this book had a co-author, it would be Angie.

Huge gratitude to all my friends and family who visited these wonderful places with me, including Sarah Libertus, Caroline Vaaler, Kit Wilson, Norah Shapiro, Stacia Goodman, Laura Pardo, Sarah Tarleton, Sandeep Patel, Anne Larsen Hooley, Mark Hooley, Robbin Larsen, Jane and Kevin Fields, and Annie Gillette Cleveland. I'm indebted to so many others who led me to to places I'd never heard of, including Rebecca Gillette, Jennifer Vogel, Julie Caniglia, Terri Sutton, Gülgün Kayim, Kelly Kegans, Kelly O'Brien, Betsey Kershaw, Kevin Hanstad, Kristin Montag, and Heid Erdrich. A special thanks to Kerri Westenberg, without whose thoughtfulness this project would not have come my way.

To the team at Emons Verlag, especially my talented and always-encouraging editor, Karen Seiger, a huge round of applause. I'd also like to thank Laura Olk for keeping me on track with all the moving parts, and to the rest of the Emons team for all their support.

To my children, Peter, Henrik and Luisa – no matter where life takes you, I hope you always carry the spirit of your hometown in your hearts. Last, but certainly not least, this book wouldn't have happened without my husband, Walter Schleisman, who joined me on more expeditions than I can count and played chauffeur so that I could take photos without having to deal with the hassle of parking. That's love.

Elizabeth Foy Larsen's stories have appeared in dozens of publications, including The New York Times, Mother Jones, Slate, Travel+Leisure, and FamilyFun. She's also the co-author of the bestselling Unbored series of family activity books, which taught her how to stop feeling like her family's office manager and enjoy exploring Minneapolis and St. Paul with her husband and three kids. A native Minnesotan, Elizabeth tries to embrace cold weather by knitting Scandinavian mittens, cross-country skiing, and taking saunas and jumping into a hole in the ice.